Ghosts in the Forest

A Father, a War, and a

Story of Survival

By Corinne Purtill

I.

On a day near the end of the twentieth century somewhere near the Laos-Cambodia border, a tiger stepped through the trees. Twigs snapped under her weight as she moved through damp, densely forested hills. At the smell of meat, she paused.

She had been here before, and the heft of her paws left unmistakable prints on soft earth. The tiger was hungry. Her kind had become scarcer across the vast breadth of the Indochinese peninsula, and so had the animals large enough to sate her hunger in a single kill. Large prey was nearby, and her haunches twitched in anticipation of the leap. A single, powerful bound, and her jaws would close around its throat, a body pinned beneath her muscled forelimbs. Her fangs would grip the neck until the animal suffocated, and stilled. Then she would drag it back to her den where she and her cubs would devour muscles and organs still warm with life.

Her ears flattened against her skull. The tiger stretched back onto her hindquarters, tensed like an arrow in a string, and released.

A razor-sharp bamboo arrow plunged into the soft tawny fur of her breast. The trip wire, a filament-thin vine, barely registered against her skin. With claws half-extended the tiger crashed to the ground. The movements of her rib cage became slower and shallower. An unseen pair of eyes waited in the trees for the death rattle.

Cambodia is a fist-shaped country that sits like a monkey's paw between the cupped hands of Thailand and Vietnam. In the northeasternmost corner of the country is Ratanakiri province, and in the northeasternmost corner of that is a 1,300-square-mile old-growth tropical rainforest called Virachey National Park that stretches to the borders of Laos and Vietnam. Clusters of bamboo as thick as redwood trunks erupt from the soil; tigers, gibbons and hundreds of other fauna live among its trees. The tree cover is dense enough to obscure the smoke from a cooking fire and to absorb the explosive *pop!* sound that bamboo makes when it burns. The soil is fertile, edible critters are plentiful and the terrain is exceptionally inaccessible. If it doesn't kill you, the forest is the perfect place to hide.

In the West, the term "national park" conjures marked trails and posted maps and ranger-guided hiking trips. These things exist to some degree at the relatively domesticated fringes of Virachey, but not in the park's wild heart. Park rangers conduct their surveys via airplane flyover. It's not a place one ends up by accident. The few people known to have ventured into this thick tropical rainforest include poachers, illegal loggers and other people counting on the trees to cover something up. This is where, in the latter half of 2004, a man named Moun, his wife and children, and a few other families were hiding from the world.

Their camp was small, just seven or eight little huts on bamboo stilts with roofs of woven banana leaves. When it was hot, the huts stayed cool, and when it was wet—which was often—they stayed mostly dry. They wore loincloths made of tree bark and had feet worn hard as leather from years of barefoot trekking. They bathed several times each day in the river and kept their hair and nails somewhat trimmed with battered machetes. They lived in the wild, but they did not live like wild men.

When they went into hiding fifteen years earlier (Moun had counted the rainy seasons since then) they were five men and six women with just a handful of small children between them. In those days they were young, strong and healthy—hungry, but strong—and when they felt themselves in danger they could break camp and leave without a second thought. Now, Moun thought, looking at three generations sprawled around the fire, hastily scooping rice and bits of roasted tiger flesh into their mouths, they were as slow-moving as an elephant herd. The children had grown, married each other in unions sealed with little more than a mutual agreement and a jar of home-brewed rice wine, and had children of their own. He entered the forest a young man, and now he was a grandfather.

He could not see the passage of time in his own face. Moun had never seen a mirror, or a photograph of himself, or any other image of his likeness besides the shimmering reflection in the river's surface before he plunged his hands through to wash. Moun was not a vain man and he did not care to look long. He saw instead the gray streaks at his friends' temples, the deepening creases at the corners of his wife's eyes, and of course the mound of earth at the edge of camp where the oldest of them lay buried. They could not live like this much longer, he knew. The end—of their time in hiding, of their lives, of something—was coming. He could feel it.

The only people on the planet he trusted lived here with him in these small houses built with their own hands. They had lost some along the way, but mostly they had grown, as they brought more babies into this refuge from the world. These children knew of no other people on earth, no sights but those of this dense arboreal kingdom. Fifteen years earlier, when Moun and his family entered this forest, they were escaping a war they had not chosen to take part in, but that had nonetheless put guns into their hands and redirected the shape of their lives. Now numbering 33 men, women and children, the group was approaching its limit. Many times he'd thought about leading them out, to make contact with something beyond the woods. *But the war,* he would think. The soldiers. My children. Whatever privations they suffered in the campsite, it was safer, less terrifying, than the war raging outside.

Of all Moun lacked in that forest, the gravest was this knowledge: There were no more occupiers. There were no more soldiers. There was no more fighting. The war ended twenty-five years ago.

Just two months later, Moun sat on a rough-hewn bench in a village of wood and grass stilt homes, a few hundred kilometers and a lifetime away from the forest that no longer imprisoned him. He wore a once-white T-shirt stained auburn with dust and sat with his forearms resting stiffly on his thighs, as though he were still conscious of the shirt's fabric against his skin. Between the first and second fingers of his left hand he held a stubby, hand-rolled cigar wrapped in a banana leaf. His dark brown eyes scanned his audience carefully, warily. Our eyes met and I smiled reflexively. He stared back, his expression unchanged in the manner of a pragmatic man who conserved his energies for when there was something to smile about.

My translator handed him a cell phone and asked if he knew what it was. Moun held up the phone , turning it carefully to examine the blue casing. He scrutinized the worn buttons, the anemic glow of its pale green screen, the unfamiliar script: N-O-K-I-A. Then he handed it back with a disinterested shrug. *"Ot tay,"* he said in Khmer, Cambodia's national language. Nope.

Moun, his wife Ath and another family from their group sat now in the same village where Ath was born some forty years earlier. Along the bench were a dozen children, from toddlers to twentysomethings, who never spoke, and two women who squatted on the wooden plank nursing babies with their floral sarongs tucked between their legs. As Moun and his friend Chalat Chakov spoke, the women and children spit green phlegm into the dust. They had all become sick at the sudden exposure to dust and unfamiliar germs.

It was December 2004. Ly Kamoun—Moun for short, pronounced a hard, fast *moon*—was about 40 years old. He had spent more than half his life in the forest as a prisoner, soldier or fugitive. In 1979, when he was about 15, he was kidnapped by the Khmer Rouge during the Maoist guerrillas' campaign to unmake Cambodia. When troops from neighboring Vietnam invaded the country, the Khmer Rouge made him a soldier. For the ten years he lived in their army, he was told that any Vietnamese soldier given the chance would kill him, eat his liver and slaughter his children. Then he and his family and friends defected. They ran away into the woods, making themselves marked men for their former army, too.

They lived in the forest for fifteen years, apparently detected or molested by no one, living off critters hunted with homemade traps and deteriorating army-issued weapons and crops they grew themselves. They built huts from bamboo. They made clothing from tree bark. They understood the natural world's power and limitations, and how utterly dependent they were upon each other.

In November 2004, they emerged from the trees and presented themselves to a tiny village in southern Laos as refugees from a war that no longer existed. Calls were made. Cambodian authorities picked them up and took them back to the villages they had fled decades before. They moved back in with family members—in one man's case, just across a red dirt path from the wooden house in which he was born. Moun and his family fled into the forest at a time when hungry people could be killed for eating food they weren't expressly permitted to eat, or for intervening when soldiers beat their children, or for refusing to marry the strangers the army chose as their spouses. Regardless of what they had been told by well-meaning people since returning to Cambodia, it was clear that they weren't quite sure what side of history they'd ended up on.

Years would pass before Moun admitted that 40 was an age he made up to end to my queries about his number of years on the planet, which struck him as irrelevant as the number of hairs on his head. He did not know, or care to know, the year of his birth. He was born of a people with no written language. No calendars or records marked the event of his arrival. As I would learn while trying to piece together the story of his life, Moun did not come from a storytelling culture. Questions about his life's chronology, and especially his feelings about those events, would be for him a constant source of bemusement, bewilderment and frustration.

That did not deter the reporters gathered at Moun's village that day, an international group that included my colleague Phann Ana, a reporter from the *Cambodia Daily* newspaper, and myself, a 24-year-old American journalist nearing the end of a yearlong stint at the country's English-language paper.

Ana found them first. He was friendly with the governor of Ratanakiri province, and after one of his regular calls to the politician, he hung up the phone and swaggered into the newsroom with the confidence of a reporter who knows he's got something good. The wires picked up his story on the holdouts, and by the time we'd taken the 20-hour truck ride north, reporters from around the world with more generous expense accounts had landed at Ratanakiri's dirt-runway airport.

We were there to turn the people shifting uncomfortably before us in cheap new clothing into stories. It almost didn't matter what they said. They were already archetypes, joining the isolated Amazon tribes and forgotten Japanese World War II soldiers in the canon of people who had managed, however briefly, to unhitch themselves from the world.

Draped around each child's neck was a *krama*, the checkered cotton scarf ubiquitous in Cambodia, and one of few personal items allowed by the Khmer Rouge decades before. The women had cut their and their children's hair into the regulation chin-length bob that twenty-five years earlier was required of all female revolutionaries. The children looked at us with the unnervingly empty gaze that survivors of the Khmer Rouge and those who have met former guerrillas call the "thousand-meter stare." Their hardness masked terror. They had grown up conditioned to fear the unfamiliar, and the preceding weeks had been an onslaught of foreign faces and situations. They seemed of another time, visibly uncomfortable in this world in which they were now expected to function.

Two men squatted in the dirt to show me how they had built fire in the forest, placing wood shavings between two pieces of bamboo and rubbing them vigorously against a third stick until the chips inside glowed an angry red. With blunt matter-of-factness they described their diet of wild chicken, mice, monkeys and the occasional tiger. They had no salt, they were quick to point out. This particular deprivation really seemed to smart.

Before these last few weeks they had never seen a telephone, a television or a car. They insisted—and we believed them—that it had been a full fifteen years since they had last encountered another person, that they kept completely to themselves that entire time, an isolated, self-sufficient society cut off from time and history.

"I was never happy in the forest. I wanted to see my family, my friends, my birthplace," Moun told me. "It's very different from before. Really, far different. People can freely exchange goods... they can buy and sell. It's amazing. I enjoy it like them, too. Nobody disturbs anyone."

Moun spoke briefly of a comrade of theirs, an older man who died four or five years earlier. Natural causes, Moun said. They buried his body without ceremony.

"Did anyone else die?" I asked.

"No," he said without hesitation.

"Did you meet anyone else in the forest?"

"No," he repeated.

Many times since, I have thought about that first meeting and wondered what it would be like to revisit that day, knowing what I later learned. Maybe I would have read unfairly into Moun's mannerisms, judging his posture as too taut, his responses too quick. Perhaps I would have felt compassion for a person who had been tested in a way few humans would wish to be. I might have looked at him differently, had I known from the beginning that the story of this gentle, soft-spoken man included starvation, violence and murder. But to understand that, one would have to look far beyond the trailing smoke of a leaf-wrapped cigar.

The first time he went to the market to choose his own clothes, Moun's eldest son came home in a baby blue baseball cap, baby blue button-up shirt and matching trousers. He blew the rest of his money on a plastic Casio wristwatch, even though he couldn't tell time.

It was overwhelming, the amount of novelty there was to contend with. When the Khmer Rouge took them from Ratanakiri, there were no phones or motorbikes. There was no currency or packaged food. There were no plastic goods or Western-style clothing, and now all of those things were as much a part of village life as the rice wine and the pigs.

Shortly after meeting Moun, Ana and I visited Romam Luong, another man who had come out of the forest with him. We found him in a village dotted with rubbish and ash piles. In his arms, he cradled like a baby a black plastic Chinese-made tape recorder. It played a tape of traditional music from the Tampuon people, his ethnic group. His face held the unguarded wonder of a child.

"I don't know what this thing is," he told us. "But I love it."

Slowly, they lost their new-penny looks. The women grew their bobs out and pinned them in the stylish updos fashionable in their village. The province's red dust stained their new clothing, just as it did everything else.

Moun built a trim wooden stilt house with a corrugated zinc roof and planted some cashew nut trees. He learned to count and use money, though the busy covered market confused him and he stayed away as much as possible. His eldest daughter divorced the young man she married in the forest and returned home with her two young children. His youngest children were in school. His family was healthy. They were alive.

I thought of Moun a lot back in the United States, where recollections of a year in Cambodia followed me through drive-throughs and municipal meetings: the woman shivering in agony in a metal-frame hospital bed after a jealous mistress doused her with battery acid, the children living against a wall of solid-packed trash and feces in a crumbling Phnom Penh cinema.

Moun's was the one I told when people asked for a story from Cambodia, and as I answered for others the questions I once asked him—What did they eat? How did they live?—I realized how much remained unanswered, and how much I still did not understand.

There was more to their survival than the simple mechanics of shelter and food. Was it really possible to live that long without any contact with the outside world, even in the Cambodian jungle? Were their motivations as simple as they'd made them out to be? Instinctively I felt there was more they hadn't told me, questions I hadn't known to ask. I just didn't know what they were.

So I went back. In January 2008, Ana picked me up at Phnom Penh International Airport. Days later we were navigating the pitted dirt road to the village of Krala, bumping along past the hypnotically tidy rows of cultivated rubber trees and squat cashew plants with their fire-colored fruits. Between cleared and cultivated ground sprouted thickets of towering vine-draped trees known as the private roaming ground of *arak*—the spirits. No axe or human hand disturbs these patches out of respect for their supernatural inhabitants, who can be moody and vindictive when their wishes are ignored.

In its dry season state, Krala was an earthy palette of auburn dirt and yellow bamboo. The small clearing of houses occupied only a bit of the expansive village of farms, cemeteries and spirit forest. As we drove to Moun's farm the landscape stretched open in wide swaths of green and brown. We parked and walked carefully so as not to crush anyone's crops, ending in a sun-baked field stripped of its tree cover.

I lifted my hand to shield my eyes and saw a man lift a weathered, much-used plastic water jug to his lips. His hair was slightly longer and a little grayer, his face less gaunt than it was four years ago, another leaf cigar clenched in his hand. There was no telephone in Krala, no postal service; we had no way to inform him we were coming. Nonetheless Moun turned and looked at us with an unhurried gaze, almost amused, as though he had been expecting us for quite some time.

He greeted Ana without looking at me and motioned us to follow. The plastic water jug bumped gently against his back as he walked. His dog Aiprip yipped at his heels. I asked Moun what use dogs were in farming.

"He doesn't do anything," he replied over his shoulder. "He's a dog."

I hadn't remembered how tiny he was, barely five feet tall, with the abbreviated limbs of one who did not have enough to eat as a child. His resin-stained trousers and frayed cotton shirt hung like dress-up clothes on a child's frame. The shirt's buttons were re-sewn with baby pink thread.

His proportions belied his voice, a rich baritone hollowed from years of tobacco and rice wine. I asked after his health. He said he was mostly fine—since coming back from the forest, he'd fallen ill twice with a cough and fever.

He didn't have money for medicine anyway, so it didn't really matter, he laughed.

"Here, it's healthier," he said. "I feel stronger than I did in the forest. We have enough to eat." He listed the benefits of village living—they could eat pork as often as once a week, compared with once every three weeks in the forest, and it could be purchased at the market or bartered from a neighbor, which was far more convenient than shooting a boar himself with a bamboo arrow. They had all the salt they needed now, Moun said, and "seasoning" (monosodium glutamate granules, imported from Vietnam and sold by the kilogram at the market). There were happy occasions to look forward to, like weddings and prayer ceremonies. He said he no owned no weapons, though it occurred to me that the scythe with which he chopped absently at the ground could certainly be used as one if the occasion arose.

The quarter-century he'd spent in the forest was little more than an unpleasant memory to him now—at least, he wanted it to be no more than that. Whatever struggles he faced in this new world, it was still infinitely better than those dark years.

"Now life is still hard," he said. "But not too hard, like it was before."

He missed his friends from the forest, he said. Luong lived less than fifteen miles away, in a village accessible by motorbike. Chakov, the other man we'd met four years earlier in Krala, lived even closer. But motorbike taxis cost money that none of them had. The families had not seen each other in four years for want of a $5 fare. Ana and I looked at each other. We could fix that.

Two days later, we picked up Luong in his village and stopped by the muddy expanse of the provincial market to purchase pork, chicken, rice and vegetables, plus a case of Angkor beer. Luong asked if we might also get a treat for his grandchildren, the offspring of his son and Moun's daughter. The couple split upon emerging from the forest, and the children had gone back to Krala with their mother. Luong strained against his seatbelt as we pulled into the village, hoping for a glimpse of the children under the eaves of Moun's house.

We parked and I hopped out of the car. I was a few yards away before a noise made me turn around. Luong was pressed helplessly against the glass, slapping at the window for assistance. I had forgotten that he didn't know how to open a car door.

As the children played with the packaging of swiftly devoured shrimp crackers, Luong lit a cigarette and talked about his hopes for their future.

"I want to teach them to be hard worker," he said. "How to tend a plant, to tend vegetables. That is a better way than being lazy. If you do less, you also have less product. That's true for any nationality. I've heard about a Khmer man from Kompong Cham who moved to a village nearby. In the beginning he was poor, but he worked hard. Now he has a big rubber plantation. If you have a cashew plantation, like I do, that's just small. But with a rubber plantation, you can get rich. You can make anything from that—buttons, cars, shoes." The former communist soldier had picked up on the basics of the market economy.

Moun arrived from the field. Within minutes a second motorbike taxi pulled up, and off stepped Chakov, the third surviving patriarch. A wiry man whose sleeve cuffs extended to the tips of his fingers, Chakov exuded a sloppy, impish air that made him seem drunk even when he wasn't.

The friends greeted each other with little more than smiles. Public displays of physical affection are almost totally absent in the indigenous ethnic minority communities in which the three men were raised—but the array of rituals surrounding animal sacrifice and wine drinking could express just as many degrees of love and hospitality.

Moun hailed from the Kreung, one of eight indigenous ethnic minority groups native to Ratanakiri. As a Kreung friend later explained to me, "For minority people, when we see someone we love very much, we have to take rice wine. Wine means, 'I greet you here. I welcome you here. I missed you very much.' And then they kill one chicken."

"Are we going to chat all day?" Moun asked upon spying my notebook. Assured that we would not, he relaxed and opened his first beer.

After lunch we sat in a circle on Moun's floor. A cloud of cigarette smoke, a heavy meal and the afternoon heat made for a languid, lazy atmosphere. Moun's eldest daughter unbuttoned her blouse and hiked up her bra so her baby could play with her nipples as she lay dozing on the floor. Ath sat near the door, listening while poised to tend to any crying children.

I passed around copies of printed photographs. *The New York Times* had just written about the Hmong, the tribal ethnic minority group in Laos that the U.S. Central Intelligence Agency paid to fight the Communists during the covert war in that country from 1961 to 1975. When the U.S. pulled out of Indochina, its former Hmong allies were left largely to fend for themselves, outnumbered by a victorious Communist government looking to settle scores.

Many retreated to the forest to survive by their wits and surreptitious donations of food and supplies from sympathetic farmers. Anywhere from a few hundred to a few thousand Hmong fighters and their families were still living in the jungle 30 years later, hiding, like Moun's family, from the repercussions of a failed war. The *Times* reporter found five hungry and frightened families living in conditions that the men gathered on the floor of Moun's house recognized instantly.

Like Moun's clan, the Hmong were an ethnic minority used to forest-based life and combat. The Hmong moved every few weeks, built bamboo huts and relied on many of the same survival techniques that Moun's family did. They differed from Moun's group in that they knew that the war was technically over, they had regular contact with settled people who knew about their existence, and their fears were justified—there were, in fact, people waiting to punish them on the outside.

The men and women scrutinized the photos with furrowed brows and worried eyes. The construction and layout of the Hmong forest homes were similar to theirs—rickety hillside houses, walls of woven bamboo—but what held their attention were the people. They could not read the words printed on the page, but the faces in the photographs telegraphed a familiar pain.

"I pity them," Luong said softly.

Together, interjecting and layering memories over one another, they gave a rough outline of their years together. They met each other sometime in the 1980s, when they were all cordoned at a Khmer Rouge camp called O'Chong. In 1989, that camp was raided by an armed contingent of Vietnamese and Cambodian government forces. The raid was meant to free the hostage populace from the Khmer Rouge and return them to their villages. The men did not know that—they believed it was an act of war—so they took off together.

After 1989, the families lived a nomadic existence. They would hike to a spot, make camp, and then remain for two to three years, surviving on food gathered from the forest and whatever they were able to grow themselves. For the first few years, they still hoped to reconnect with other soldiers or people they knew at O'Chong. But after many seasons, their hopes hardened into paranoia and they felt safe with no one. The sight of an unfamiliar footprint or a tree no one remembered cutting was enough to make them break camp and move on. They were afraid to risk contact with anyone—they could be arrested, or worse. But they never considered splitting up, even if the size of their camp increased the risk of detection. Whatever their weaknesses, they knew that they were stronger together than apart.

"If we lived separately, it would be even scarier," Luong said.

Life was not all bad in the forest, he said. They celebrated their children's weddings, drank home-brewed rice wine. Their spiritual practices were a peculiar hybrid of traditional animism and the enforced atheism of the Khmer Rouge. They acknowledged the existence of spirits in the forest as plainly as they did the presence of trees or rocks, and said they often warned fussy children that evil spirits were watching their bad behavior. But they did not think of themselves as religious. Their brand of animism emphasizes practice over personal belief. To Moun, it was the physical trappings of faith—animal sacrifices, gongs and spirit healers—that counted as "religion." Without those things in the forest, they said, they had no spiritual life.

"There was no prayer in the forest, but we had a lot of rice," Moun had told me. "Now, we pray but there's no rice!" he said, breaking into a big laugh.

Surely there must have been moments of terrible despair. After ten, fifteen, twenty years passed with no promise of rescue, I asked, were they ever tempted to give up? Did they ever consider suicide, even at their lowest point? On this point, every one in the room forcefully agreed: absolutely not. Suicide was a crime committed not against the self, but against those who had to contend with the dead person's vengeful, reckless spirit afterward. As soon as a person dies, he or she becomes a spirit, a being with its own personality that may not bear any similarity to the living person it once was.

With suicide, the unnatural manner of death means that the spirit is forever tormented—and a tormented spirit is very dangerous to the living. Some indigenous communities bury those who die by their own hand far away from the village cemetery, so as to protect the living and the dead from the wrath of an angry soul.

"If we are suffering and we kill ourselves, we hang ourselves, then we have nothing," Luong said. "We would end everything, but more importantly, other people would regard us as a bad person. As the worst person. It's very cowardly."

Only one person in their group died during their whole time in the forest, they said—a man who was married to the elegant-looking woman now sitting next to Ath in Moun's doorway. They rarely discussed this man. A scouring of my notes later yielded not even a mention of his name. For someone who had worked, laughed, struggled and suffered alongside them for years, he was acutely absent from their recollections. All I knew was that he died of *jamneu lewang*, the disease of no energy.

It seemed that way with so many things in their lives—belongings, children, opportunities, freedom. They enjoyed it while it was present, but once it was gone, it was gone, with no longing, grieving or resentment. It seemed like a defense against a world where babies could get sick, drought could destroy your crop, war could break out, and suddenly the future you were counting on was gone.

I wanted to make a list of all the people who had lived in the forest: men, women and children. I thought it was a simple enough question: If you saw the same handful of people every day for two decades, presumably you'd have no trouble remembering their names. To my surprise, it elicited a long round of heated discussion that even Ana had trouble keeping track of.

The conversation shifted from Khmer to Kreung. The women chimed in. Adults began counting on their fingers. The room got louder as people interrupted each other. There were only a few dozen of them, I thought—should this be taking so long?

"And then there was the other boy, Lan, but he was arrested with the other families," Moun said.

Arrested?

Sometime in the 1990s nine people were arrested, the men calmly explained: two women and seven children. Police had discovered their camp, for some reason—on this point, they were vague— and surrounded them. Two women, one of them pregnant, were unable to run away. Assuming that the police were going to kill the pair, the group took their children at their request and left the women behind. Two of those children later died in the forest.

Moun, Luong and the others always assumed those women were slaughtered immediately. It was only after they came home in 2004 and the women visited them that they realized the pair had actually been saved.

"We worried that they would be killed because we had lived in the forest so long, and perhaps the soldiers thought that we were traitors. But then they got to Banlung [the provincial capital] and they were happier and luckier than us," Moun said.

Then they moved on, abandoning the discussion and chatting sleepily among themselves.

In all the time we had spent with the various returnees, no one had ever mentioned an arrest. They'd always maintained the same story—*four families went in, four families came out, and we never saw anyone in between.* Now it was clear that there was more to their tale. How had authorities—police, soldiers, it wasn't clear who—stumbled upon their remote settlement? Who were these other women? What happened to them? And was Moun saying that they had left some of their children behind to be raised by the group in the forest, and these children were the only ones to die? The story didn't feel whole. I started to wonder what other secrets they held.

"Why didn't you talk about this before?" I said.

"You didn't ask," Moun replied.

The conversation broke up. Moun went off on an errand. Luong and Chakov chatted with each other, laughing and talking over private memories. Moun's 12-year-old son Theang swung in the hammock below the house, fiddling studiously with Ana's phone. Over and over again the phone chirped the melody of "Rhythm of the Rain": "Listen to the rhythm of the falling rain/Telling me just what a fool I've been…."

Some highlanders hang pieces of wasp nest in the doorway of their homes as a deterrent to evil spirits. The idea is that the malevolent spirit will pause on its way into the house to count the holes in the nest, lose count, start again, grow frustrated, and eventually leave to bother another family. Seated on Moun's stoop, my dirt- and sweat-streaked face cupped in my hands, I didn't know whether to sympathize with the homeowner or the spirit.

33

There were only four families—except there were more. Nobody died in all that time—except for an old man and two children. **The Khmer Rouge uprooted thousands of families. Almost none had disappeared for as long as this clan.** I had the uneasy feeling that the facts of their story were obscured by more than the fog of time.

I looked up. Moun was hiking across the village, wearing the biggest grin he'd had all day and carrying a giant ceramic jar of rice wine on his shoulder. Whatever the truth was, it wasn't going to get told today.

Ana went back to his job in Phnom Penh a week later. After auditioning a raft of potential translators who evoked the bad-date montages of B-movies, I met Sotheara, a 21-year-old Kreung man. An aspiring doctor forced to quit school for lack of fees, his bookish inclinations made him something of a village oddball.

"I am the laziest!" he said, laughing, as we sat with bowls of rice noodle soup in a wooden café in Banlung. "I don't want to do anything. I don't like to work in the farm. It's too hot. Inside the school, it's easy. It's not hot. Reading and writing is my favorite thing. My family call me lazy, and I totally agree with them. School is my happy place."

We went to Krala the next day and chanced upon the wedding celebrations of the village chief's son. The ceremony itself had already taken place, culminating in the ritual slaughter of a buffalo; the ensuing party was a raucous affair that would last all through that night and well into the next day.

Smoke from dozens of cooking fires outside filled the bamboo meeting hall and mingled with clouds of tobacco. The bride, a pretty girl in her late teens, watched the festivities from a hammock in the corner. The room reverberated with gongs and drums and the shouts of people in various states of inebriation. The whole village seemed to be there— except for Moun.

I wanted to talk to the bride, to know what her thoughts were as she watched the first hours of a new stage of her life play out. I wanted to talk to the milky-eyed elderly woman with a possessive grip on the rice wine straw, to understand what she had seen and lost. At the barbecue at Moun's house, the susurrus of the women's private conversations in Kreung encircled the men's translated discussion. I longed to hear their stories. When I asked them questions, they smiled and waved me off.

A few years after the families came out of the forest, a journalist from a women's magazine came to Ratanakiri to write about them. She interviewed Moun's wife and daughters, noting the "strange tricks" that forest life played on the aging process: "Mother-of-seven At, 39, resembles an old woman—but her daughters . . . look far younger than their years." The writer accompanied the girls to the Banlung market, where they went bra shopping, got their hair done and talked about how they met their husbands. ("My husband, Kyong, was the only male near my age I wasn't related to, so I knew it had to be him," Moun's daughter-in-law said of her marriage. "Luckily, he liked me.")

Ana had worked as her translator. Years later, he was still scarred by the experience.

"She want to know about the women—about their hygiene, how they love," Ana said, stubbing out the first cigarette of the morning and shuddering at the memory. "I don't want to ask about these things! Very difficult for me."

"How do Khmer women have babies?" I asked.

"I don't know about that!" he said reproachfully. "I just stand outside, pound on the door, ask, 'Is my wife okay?' I don't know about these things." He shook his head, straightened his shoulders and lit another cigarette. Conversation over.

Subsequent translators—all male—shared this reluctance to delve into women's lives. The only people in Ratanakiri who had been to school to learn English were men, who then spoke to other men about the things men were interested in. On every visit to Krala the women greeted me politely and then ignored the ensuing conversation, their attention consumed by the children, the household, the meals, the neighbors. Men were responsible for labor-intensive but less-frequent jobs like cutting trees and building houses; women tackled the daily grind of keeping a household running. The work was hard. Women in Krala had bulging biceps.

I did not get the impression that the women in Moun's family were silenced. Highlander societies gave women the upper hand in finances, divorces, spouse selection and names, and these women were not shrinking violets. Talking to a foreigner was simply another chore better delegated to men. This was fine with everyone but me. In the villages I felt like the sole inhabitant of a weird, genderless no-person's-land, with none of the authority of a man or the capability of a woman. In the in-between times when Moun and my translator shared pleasantries in Kreung, sometimes with Theang perched inquisitively nearby, I watched his wife and daughters talk and joke with one another as they went about their work, and longed to connect with them. They kept the history I wanted to understand.

We left the wedding and made our way to Moun's house. His eldest daughter told us her father was out clearing a new crop field, about a mile's walk away. Theang volunteered to take us.

The soles of his much-repaired sandals flopped against the dirt.

As the morning's cool burned away, the boy stripped off his shirt like a seasoned laborer. With an *ah!* of excitement, he plucked a sprig of rose-colored berries from a nearby branch and popped the sweet treats into his mouth.

The trees grew closer together; the path all but disappeared under the brush. We edged across bamboo planks laid down over creek and up dirt footholds hacked into steep hillsides. Soon the hollow, repetitive thwack of axe against wood came beating through the trees. From a distance I saw a lean, muscular man in a baseball cap chopping at a tree trunk with a bamboo-handled axe. Moun turned and smiled.

He was wearing a lime-green polo shirt intended for a woman that he'd purchased from the provincial market for 500 riel, or about 13 cents. He had recently acquired the rights to farm this plot of land, and today he was clearing away the trees and brush.

A ring of thick trees the height of three-story buildings encircled the perimeter of the lot, with notches cut about one-third of the way through each trunk. With a final, powerful swing, he sank the axe into the last tree and sat down on the crunchy carpet of fallen leaves.

The farm was Moun's primary concern. It was the sole source of his family's income and the place where he spent the majority of his waking hours. It was the reason that he was out here working alone, instead of at the wedding where the rest of his village was currently getting drunk. Cashew trees take years to bear saleable fruit, and Moun always felt like he was behind. The addition of this second field would help his income, but getting started was a challenge. Clearing trees was taxing work, and with his only grown son off tending his own field, Moun was on his own.

Moun lit a cigarette and spoke to us of his childhood. He was born in a village called Kalai, he told us, at a time when people still built their houses amidst big trees and wore traditional clothes. His father still lived in that village, which was not so far from here. Khmer Rouge soldiers kidnapped him while he was gathering cassava "when I was as small as him," he said, pointing at Theang. He never saw his mother again.

Moun was a soldier for most of his life, from his conscription as a child to the moment when he and his family emerged from the forest in 2004. It was difficult to imagine this soft-spoken, self-effacing man at war.

Had he ever killed anyone?

Moun looked at the ground. "Yes," he said. "I killed people."

As we talked, Theang amused himself with his father's axe and his broken flip-flop. He practiced chopping down trees, imitating Moun in the way boys back home lathered up their faces to mimic their father's shaving. He scratched his back with Moun's machete, lolled about in the leaves, chased dragonflies through the trees.

Moun had had no father to model himself after as a young man. All the father figures that the village would have provided were lost to him with his kidnapping. One of the hardest parts of forest life, he said, was being forced into the role of elder without the requisite age and experience. He didn't want that for his son.

"When Theang is older, I will teach him about farming, about our culture," Moun said. "When he's 16, 17. An adult. That's the time when men can take care of themselves, work on their own farm, get married. They don't need their father anymore.

"I don't want my son to be like me," he said. "Maybe in the future there will be no more forest, no more land to farm. I want my son to have a good job, maybe in the government."

Here Theang lost interest in the discussion. Taking Moun's axe, he picked up a thick piece of bark and casually hacked it into the shape of a rifle.

There was an arresting sound—the crackle of the trees at the perimeter of the field, a staccato *rat-tat-tat* that grew into a roar. I looked up to see the tree where Moun had left his axe pitch drunkenly to its side and collapse into its neighbor. That tree, too, snapped at the place where Moun had cut his mark, and crashed into the tree next to it. One after another, they fell like giant dominoes. The forest was collapsing around us in an explosion of leaves and dirt and falling branches. *What a strange way this is to die*, I thought.

In seconds, it was over. The overgrown patch of jungle was flattened. We sat in the center of a circle of splayed trees, each of which had been cut at precisely the right angle to take out its neighbor. Falling leaves drifted confetti-like to the ground.

No one I asked later recognized this method of clearing trees as a traditional Kreung technique. I've found no evidence of its practice elsewhere. Moun invented it himself, a clever scheme designed by a man with a lot of work to do and no one to help him.

I looked at him. He laughed, this diminutive man with the power to make the trees do his bidding.

Later that day I sat at a table at the open-air restaurant of the Tribal Hotel in the Banlung nursing a *tuk krouch ma*—lime juice—and thinking about Moun. The gentle character now peacefully tending his cashew trees had lived through circumstances that did not favor the meek. His story included a childhood uprooted by war, conscription into a brutal army, a coming of age amid violence and fear. Survival is a messy, unforgiving business. One could not live through all that Moun had by accident.

Moun was not one for self-reflection—his culture is one that seeks guidance externally in the family, the village, and the forest-village-spirit cosmology that dictates one's place in the world. If I wanted to understand the secrets of Moun's survival, I would also need to explore those worlds to comprehend how a boy who grew up in the fields could fight—and kill—to stay alive.

I thought of a conversation I'd had earlier with Mony, the young manager hired to help at the Tribal when the owner's husband fell ill. The sick man, a diabetic, was a beloved character who lavished affection on Mony's young family, even when paralyzed and bedridden in the final years of his life.

"He loved my children! He loved my husband. He was so nice," Mony said wistfully.

Then she shook her head. "But we say in Cambodia, the nice people never live long. When you live long, you have to fight with life. Nice people cannot."

II.

Moun does not know the year he was born in Kalai village, a Ratanakiri hamlet enclosed by tall, shady trees. If he was like most Kreung babies, he spent his first few days in his mother's arms during her *koo pung oing*, the Kreung term that means "sitting on the fire." While Moun nursed and slept, his mother's female relatives placed hot stones on her belly so that the heat would seep into her body and restore her strength. Moun spent these days naked and diaperless. When he was a few days old, a villager slathered the paste of a root called *jarou shrabu* on his fontanel. Babies are especially vulnerable to *shrabu*, the Kreung word for diseases that come from the outside, as opposed to those arising internally. *Shrabu* could be carried in by the wind and burrow into a baby's body, particularly through the vulnerable soft spot on its head. *Shrabu* could cause untold suffering. Within a week or two, his mother rose from the hut, tied Moun in a cloth sling around her shoulders, and went back to work in the fields.

For the first year of his life Moun lived in near-constant contact with his mother's skin. When she worked, he rested against her back in a sling; when he cried, she twisted the cloth around to the front to nurse. In his sling he bounced along as his mother walked between the tall dipterocarp trees of the forest, looking for shoots and tubers that she dug from the ground with her hands, and at home he felt the heat of the cooking fire as she prepared them for dinner.

When Moun stood on his own for the first time, this is what the ground felt like beneath his feet: hard-packed soil, swept smooth by the poundings of many feet and the brush of banana-leaf brooms, grit squirming into the crevices as his toes gripped the earth.

Moun was part of the region's indigenous ethnic minorities, known collectively as highlanders. Divided among eight different ethnic groups, the highlanders of Ratanakiri are among Cambodia's first peoples, akin to the Native American tribes in North America or the Aborigines of Australia. It isn't clear where their ancestors emigrated from or how they came to live in the hilly region that spans the confluence of Cambodia, Vietnam and Laos. Anthropologists have found terms in the languages of highland tribes in Vietnam that refer to woolly mammoths, giant sloths and hippopotami, all of which have been extinct in their region for millennia. The highlanders, however, are not big on record-keeping. All their myths are oral. They have no written language. The past is fine and all, but what is really important is the world as it is, right now.

In the dry season, the powder-fine dust of Ratanakiri was everywhere, burrowing its way into the carved grooves of rice wine jars, the crannies in baskets' bamboo weaves, the ears and nostrils of little boys. During the day pigs and chickens pecked across the ground nibbling at scraps and dried rice crusts, and at night the men shooed their cows and buffaloes into the village center to sleep. The animals left tarry black plops of dung on the ground that Moun had to watch for in the morning.

When the rains arrived in May, the daily downpours swept away the heat and dust, restoring a brilliant green luster to the leaves. The clouds rolled in every afternoon, regular almost to the minute, preceded by a wind carrying the rustling sound of every leaf in the forest. The heavy drops exploded with force against the ground, as though rain were shooting up from the earth as well as down upon it.

In the evenings the village grew dark quickly. Families sat around their cooking fires, talking softly, and retired early to rise with the sun. Moun's family slept together on the floor of their home. He woke each morning at the rooster's cry with the weave of his sleeping mat impressed faintly on his skin.

It was good to be a boy in Kalai. Boys had it easier than girls, who started pounding rice and feeding chickens when they were 6 years old and started acting bossy before they had hips. Young boys Moun's age were mostly expected to stay out of the way of people with more important work to do. There were only a handful of schools in Ratanakiri province, and no one expected that he should attend one.

He watched his mother dig for roots and mushrooms in the forest, saw her build the fire and boil wild greens to go with their rice for dinner. He saw her choose plants that were edible and avoid those that were not. He watched his father gut fish, silver scales flashing against the quick motions of his knife. In the dry season Moun prowled the riverbeds, flipping over rocks in search of tiny fish or crabs living in the damp pools beneath. In the humid months when grown-ups were busy in the fields, he tramped through the forest unsupervised, plucking fruits off the trees and devouring them in big greedy bites. The juice dribbled down his chin, leaving sticky trails on his dusty face.

A fence of bamboo posts enclosed the entire village, demarcating the border between Kalai and the forest where tigers and other predatory animals stalked. Elephants could dash houses with their trunks and crush a man with a single step. Mothers in Kalai did not allow their children to wander far from the village alone. For safety, people traveled in groups to their crop fields outside the village bounds. They carried crossbows and poison-tipped darts.

Deadly animals notwithstanding, the forest surrounding Kalai was shelter, grocery and general store. Hardly any of Cambodia's currency circulated in Moun's village, and there was no need for it when everything a person needed was available for the taking. When it was time to build a house, the men cut down a tree. For food, one planted, gathered, scavenged or hunted. If someone got sick, the right combination of shoots, bark or leaves could fix any problem from cramps to malaria, and if that didn't work, there would be an animal sacrifice, and if that didn't work, then it was simply time to die, and the village would bury you properly and ensure that your spirit was placated.

Moun could look ahead and see all of the stages of his life unfold before him. There were the confident young unmarried men setting out for the hunt, pranking each other by setting small fires in their wake so that stragglers couldn't catch up to the party. There were the men like his father, clearing trees and consulting one another on matters of farm and village, collectively maintaining order and justice. There were the old men, squatting on their heels, smoking and watching the world with milky eyes. Even the spirits had their place in Kalai, in the overgrown spirit forests that no human hand dared cut.

All were essential organs of the being that was the village. Around the warmth of his family's campfire at night, there was no way for Moun to know that he was born at the wrong time in history, and how soon all this would end.

Of all the communist movements that swept Southeast Asia in the 1960s and '70s, none were as bloody as Cambodia's. More Maoist than Mao, driven by ideology uncoupled from reality, the Khmer Rouge destroyed their country in a futile quest for an agrarian utopia. The regime worked people to death in pursuit of wildly unrealistic production goals and purged anyone perceived as an obstacle to their ends. Between 1975 and 1979, one fifth of the nation's population died as a a result of overwork, starvation, disease and execution.

The Khmer Rouge came to power as victors of a bloody five-year civil war between the forces of Lon Nol, a U.S.-backed leader of a coup d'état against Prince Norodom Sihanouk, and a coalition army of communist and royalist troops. When the Khmer Rouge finally toppled Lon Nol's government and marched into Phnom Penh on April 17, 1975, citizens lined the streets and cheered. Though they knew nothing about these new leaders, and the dead eyes of these boy soldiers unsettled many citizens watching the parade that day, they were optimistic that victory meant they could finally get on with their lives.

Within hours of taking Phnom Penh, the Khmer Rouge announced to the world that Cambodia was now Democratic Kampuchea, a new country with a new constitution. Foreigners were evicted. The borders were sealed. Young Khmer Rouge cadres drove the streets of Phnom Penh with megaphones, ordering residents to leave their homes and march, in triple-digit temperatures, into the countryside. There were no more cities, no more businesses, no more clerks or shopkeepers. Everyone worked now for the Khmer Rouge.

Nineteen seventy-five, the new regime announced, was Year Zero. They wanted to start over, to transport the nation back to the idyllic scenes carved on the sides of the temples at Angkor Wat, when Khmers were in charge and their power seemed limitless. "If our people were capable of building Angkor," said Khmer Rouge leader Pol Pot in one of his rare public speeches, "they can do anything."[1] Cambodia needed to be torn down and rebuilt from the ground up, so that an enlightened new era could begin.

Under *Angka*—the "organization," the Khmer Rouge's name for the all-encompassing, omnipresent state—money, markets and private property were abolished. Phnom Penh's massive yellow-domed Central Market, once a bustling center of urban life, became an empty shell. Schools and monasteries were shuttered. Publishing was forbidden. The postal system was shut down. Travel was restricted. Men, women and children

[1] David Chandler, *Brother Number One: A Political Biography of Pol Pot,*

were allowed to dress only in the national uniform of black work shirt and trousers, with a checkered *krama*, or cotton scarf, knotted about the neck. People tainted by imperialist institutions—the educated, the religious, employees of the previous regime, and anyone of a different ethnicity—were executed. *To keep you is no benefit,* went one of *Angka's* oft-repeated maxims. *To kill you is no loss.*

The Khmer Rouge systematically targeted families, the bedrock of Cambodian society. Family mealtimes were abolished and replaced with communal mess halls. Men and women were split into single-sex dormitories, and children were separated from parents. They were also encouraged to spy on their families and report disloyal behavior such as sneaking food, in many cases sentencing their parents to death. Fear subsumed the most basic human instincts. One survivor told me that his mother watched silently as he was struck with an axe and beaten after picking grass to feed his pregnant sister. She was too afraid to cry.

Once in Ratanakiri, when talking with a group of men who had all been married in mass ceremonies to wives pre-selected for them by the Khmer Rouge, the usually unflappable Ana stood abruptly and left the restaurant, where he lit a cigarette and stared at the dirt road. When he finally spoke again, his voice was thick with emotion.

"Your heart, your head, your hair, your body, your soul—all belong to the organization," he said, each word a soft blow. "In this way, it is like a god. You, yourself, does not really belong to you." The Khmer Rouge executed Ana's father and left his body in a compost pile for his 7-year-old son to find.

It was from the jungles of Ratanakiri that Pol Pot planned his revolution in secret in the late 1960s. He liked the protection that the forest cover offered, and he liked the highlanders, with their collective society and history of fearless performance in battle. Thanks to years of mistreatment and exploitation, many of them also harbored a burning hatred of the same government the communists wished to overthrow. The

American B-52 bombing campaign that destroyed villages and left gruesome scars on land and psyches also helped propel the highlanders toward the Khmer Rouge.

It did not take long before the highlanders grew disillusioned with these rulers as well. The Khmer Rouge confiscated the gongs and rice wine jars used in animist ceremonies. They marched highlanders into spirit forests they believed forbidden to human visitors and forced them to eat foods traditionally considered taboo. They discouraged traditional swidden farming practices, the mainstay of highlander life, and pressured them to cultivate wet rice paddies like lowland Khmer instead.

I once spoke to a Kreung man named Nieng Ta. American warplanes started dropping B-52 bombs on his village in 1973, when Ta was about 16. His family and neighbors fled into the forest to hide from the fiery shells exploding over their homes. His father died of illness while the family was in hiding. Ta understood that Khmer Rouge forces were fighting the people who dropped these bombs, and in 1974 he enlisted. His legs, arms and torso were flecked with keloid scars, evidence of a land mine explosion that killed six people and left him the only survivor.

Pol Pot was not all bad, Ta said. In fact, in those early years, the Khmer Rouge really had it right. They encouraged Cambodians to take back their country from a corrupt leader. From the Khmer Rouge, the former soldier said, highlanders learned how to operate as a society, to work as a team toward a goal. They became harder workers. Pol Pot never sold land illegally, the way Cambodia's leaders do today, he said.

It was only after the Khmer Rouge won, only after they took over the country in 1975, that everything changed. First it was little stuff. Soldiers were supposed to get rice porridge at breakfast and a more substantial meal of rice at lunch and dinner; soon, their meals consisted only of rice porridge. People starved. The purges started. If the Khmer Rouge hadn't killed so many people back then, Ta said, there would be more people alive today to help their communities. And they took people's children away from them.

Ta blamed lower-level cadres for most of the suffering; he still thinks that Pol Pot had some good ideas. But he could not forgive Pol Pot for selling out on his promise to give highlanders a better life.

"I was very happy when the Khmer Rouge won against Lon Nol," he said. "But from 1975 on, the Khmer Rouge changed. Pol Pot was not honest."

The Khmer Rouge killed so many of their own people that they didn't have enough to keep the experiment going. They needed new recruits, and none were better than children: uncorrupted by society, malleable, unopinionated and naturally inclined to trust authority.   "Only children can purely serve the revolution and eliminate reactionism, since they are young, obedient, local and active," said Ieng Thirith, Democratic Kampuchea's Minister of Culture and Social Affairs. (Though she had no problem making soldiers of other people's children, Ieng Thirith made sure her four children had comfortable jobs in the medical corps near her home.)

The ideal child was "clean cut," meaning no formal education or ties to foreign or bourgeois enemies. This made the vulnerable children of the rural provinces prime candidates for conscription. *Angka* made all the decisions, and *Angka* decided that it was acceptable for a child to fight, and to die.

On the last morning of his life as a child, Moun joined a group of young people heading to the forest to forage for the day's vegetables. It was the rainy season, sometime between May and October, 1979, and his feet sunk into rich red mud. Moun was around 14 years old. He was smaller than other boys his age. He was shy.

The children wound through the trees, walking farther from Kalai in search of a field not yet picked over, finally settling on a site too far for their voices to carry back to the village. The children set their baskets down on the ground and got to work, kneeling in the mud to look for the telltale shoots pointing to a protein-rich tuber beneath the soil.

He heard shouting, and then screaming. A man appeared—not really a man, a boy who looked just a few years old than Moun himself—and jabbed him in the stomach with the butt of his gun so hard that Moun doubled over and fought the urge to vomit. The man grabbed Moun by the arm and dragged him away. Moun did not know where they were taking him. He was so small, and so afraid, and he knew there was nothing he was physically capable of doing to this man that would stop this terrible thing.

Other boys fought and kicked. One of the men raised his gun and a boy was on the ground, his eyes open wide to the sky as the mud grew dark and sticky with his blood. There was another bang; another boy collapsed. A soldier took a stick and bashed one screaming boy against the side of his head until the boy was still and his head was like the neck of a buffalo after a sacrifice. Moun did not know people did this to each other. He turned his eyes away and fixed them on the back of the boy in front of him, who was following the soldier ahead. He never saw his mother again.

They walked for a day through a forest chalk-thick with humidity to a child labor camp called Ko Ma, where Moun and the other new recruits were given black uniform shirts. Moun had never worn a shirt before. The fabric felt hot and scratchy against his skin. Soldiers shouted at him in Khmer and he frantically copied the other boys' actions so that they didn't yell at him more for not following orders. He picked up pieces of their language: *baat* (yes), *ot tey* (no), and *Angka*, the name of the organization that ran this place, the replacement for his parents, his village. At night, the boys slept side by side in long lines next to each other on the floor. A man they were told to call "teacher" patrolled the bunks at night to make sure no one ran away.

Moun was assigned to a brick-making team. The dust coated his face and arms; it burrowed into his eyes, nose, ears and lungs. At night, after a long day of brick making and a dinner of thin rice gruel that barely slaked his hunger, Moun sat in long rows with the other boys for hours while cadres lectured about the revolution. They led songs and Moun mouthed along: "We, the children, love *Angka* with no bounds/ Because of *Angka*, we live and grow up with good health." Half the time Moun did not understand what they were saying. He did understand that he was supposed to think of *Angka* as his mother and his father, that *Angka* was making him do this work so that Cambodia could become a powerful country. If the boys saw people do subversive things, like taking food when they were not supposed to, they were to report them to superiors. Thinking of oneself, or of one's family, undermined the revolution. One should emulate Comrade Ox, the hero of an oft-recited parable: *Comrade Ox never refused to work. Comrade Ox was obedient. Comrade Ox did not complain. Comrade Ox did not object when his family was killed.*[2]

Moun was hungry all the time. Though he could certainly have found something to eat in the

[2] Alex Hinton, "Agents of Death: Explaining the Cambodian Genocide in Terms of Psychological Dissonance," *Searching for the Truth*, Number 32, August 2002, p. 38.

forest to supplement his meager rations, he was not allowed to look for it. All food belonged to Angka, and those who forgot that were made into examples through beatings, or worse. Boys caught eating roots or leaves salvaged from the woods were pummeled until their arms hung crooked. Stragglers were tied to trees and left out in the sun as a warning to not be late for work. Children went to the infirmary with skin infections and malaria and cholera and diarrhea, and most of them never came back. Death, and the fear of death, lived alongside them.

Moun would forget what he did to deserve them, but never the beatings themselves. Nor would he forget the friends who snuck him food. He credited these acts of bravery for his survival, and remembered them with deepest gratitude.

In December 1978, after years of border skirmishes with its increasingly hostile neighbor, Vietnam invaded Cambodia. The Vietnamese army ousted the Khmer Rouge, seizing the capital on January 7, 1979. The Khmer Rouge were so taken by surprise that Vietnamese soldiers discovered the bloodied bodies of the last torture victims still chained to their beds in Phnom Penh's S-21 prison.

For most Cambodians, the Vietnamese invasion was a kind of salvation. People took to the roads by the tens of thousands, free for the first time in years to travel in search of lost loved ones, homes, villages, lives. "I want to die in the place I was born,"[3] one 83-year-old survivor of the genocide told a journalist. She was among the lucky ones. By 1979, one fifth of the nation's 1975 population was dead. Another 500,000 people had already escaped to Vietnam or Thailand. Many survivors of the Khmer Rouge's cruelties would not outlive the deprivations of the months and years ahead. In the chaos people abandoned whatever meager crops they were growing, dooming the all-important rice harvest that was the country's primary source of nourishment. More than 2 million Cambodians faced famine in 1979. Hungry refugees broke into the granaries where the Khmer Rouge stockpiled rice for export while their people starved.

---

[3] William Shawcross, *The Quality of Mercy*, 317.

In a few instances, angry mobs descended upon unlucky Khmer Rouge soldiers separated from their units and tore them apart in violent retaliation. One group of villagers dragged a particularly despised mid-level security chief from his home, tied him up, beat him and burned him to death. This particular man had a reputation for eating his victims' livers; even his wife shrugged at the news and suggested that he had it coming. But these were mostly isolated incidents. Cambodians had seen enough of death. "After so much horror, people were sick of blood," wrote Pol Pot's biographer, Philip Short. "The little energy they had left they needed for their own survival."

The world did not hail the Vietnamese as liberators. This was only four years after the United States was forced to beat a retreat from its embassy in Saigon, and the conventional wisdom was that even the presence of a genocidal regime like the Khmer Rouge was preferable to Vietnamese domination of Indochina. "You should also tell the Cambodians that we will be friends with them," Secretary of State Henry Kissinger told the Thai foreign minister in 1975, shortly after receiving the first reports of Khmer Rouge atrocities. "They are murderous thugs, but we won't let that stand in our way." With U.S. support, Democratic Kampuchea retained Cambodia's seat at the United Nations well after the Vietnamese takeover.

Buoyed by international support, the Khmer Rouge refused to accept defeat. The army headed for the Thai border, where they planned to regroup and take back their country. They forced 100,000 civilians and low-level conscripts along with them on their march into exile. One of these unlucky people was Moun. Before they left the labor camp Ko Ma, Moun was given a gun: a Kalashnikov rifle, which he called an *ah-kah*. He did not know he had just been conscripted into a defeated army.

Thus began a period of his life that Moun later described in Khmer as "pi baaq *na*"—*so* hard, harder than anything that came before. The chaotic, dangerous journey to the Thai border took the better part of a year. They marched north, then west. He walked for days that turned into weeks, his gun pressing heavily and uncomfortably into his shoulder. They were walking into the most heavily mined part of the country, away from the peace slowly dawning over Cambodia and toward the twilight of endless war.

All around him, soldiers died. The Khmer Rouge offered only one way to live, yet now, as their failed state disintegrated, there were endless ways to die. Men stepped on land mines and were torn to pieces; they crossed rivers they couldn't swim and drowned; they died of malaria; they died of hunger; they died of thirst.

Moun understood that the Vietnamese invaded Cambodia because the Vietnamese were vicious and greedy, and that his army was heading to the other side of the country to reorganize and come back stronger than ever. Moun did not know that there were highlander men from villages not far from his own who were fighting alongside the Vietnamese to throw the Khmer Rouge from power, and to reclaim life as they knew it. For the second time in a decade, highlanders were at the front lines of revolution, having sided first with the Khmer Rouge to drive an oppressive government off their land and now with the Vietnamese to topple the Khmer Rouge.

Moun was about 15 years old and caught between these generations of warriors. He carried a gun and walked across the country because the Khmer Rouge told him that the Vietnamese would gut him like a fish if they found him. He walked because the Khmer Rouge would have killed him if he stopped walking, or if he was too slow, or if he refused to go with them. He walked because he didn't think he had anything to go back to. He walked because it was deeply shameful to kill oneself on purpose, and because he was too young and strong to kill himself the quiet way, by simply giving up and letting the hunger, exhaustion and futility take over. He walked because someone told him to, and he was still a child, so he obeyed.

After many months the soldiers reached the Dangrek Mountain range. For a time they camped at the base of the mountain on which sits the Preah Vihear temple, one of the most sacred sites in Cambodia. Moun did not care. At night he shifted in his hammock looking for sleep, and his imagination did not soar upward toward the mountaintop temple. These people were not his people, and their god was not his god.

Not long after that, Moun's unit set up camp along the border with Thailand. Three years in this miserable section of tropical forest passed in a blur of sore feet, hunger, mosquito bites and battle. There was hardly any food, because the units never stayed in one place long enough to plant crops. It was hard, and hungry, and boring.

Sometimes Moun thought of his family back home, of his parents and his brother Huon. The Khmer Rouge told him that the Vietnamese were killing civilians, that they cut out people's livers and ate them to absorb their strength. When the time finally came to lift his gun in battle and fire it at another man, it was not as hard as it might once have been to kill.

In the early 1980s Moun's unit hiked back across the country. They settled in a section of forest in Stung Treng province known as O'Chong, named after the closest river. Despite the remote location and the prevalence of leeches during the rainy season, it was not a bad place to live. Fish swam in the lucid, rocky pools of the nearby stream. The surrounding forest was full of civet cats, gaur, gibbons and other wildlife. After a few weeks Moun discovered to his delight that his brother Huon was also stationed there. Married with two daughters, Huon served the Khmer Rouge as a nurse, administering traditional herbs and imported Chinese medicines to sick and wounded people. The brothers rarely spent time together in the camp, but Moun felt better just knowing he was alive and close.

The camp started with just a few families. Within a few years, it grew to a settlement of roughly two thousand people, all highlanders from a variety of ethnic groups: Kreung, Kavet, Brao, Jarai. Moun spent ten years at O'Chong. It was difficult land to farm, but crops were easily supplemented with plentiful plants and animals in the nearby forest. The camp's inhabitants lived in bamboo houses they built themselves of materials pulled from the woods.

By the time he moved to O'Chong, Moun was well practiced in the art of forest living. He knew that the first year was always a lean and hungry one as he planted seeds and waited for the first crops to come in. He knew how to scavenge for food in the meantime, and that the quality and availability of food differed based on the type of terrain. The ecosystems of the forest varied widely, and no two campsites yielded the same conditions. Understanding how to live in these different environments was a process of trial and error.

It was a home, but not quite. For one, there was no salt.

Highlander people I spoke to regularly counted the absence of salt alongside death and bombing as the worst of their sufferings under Pol Pot. Salt is the difference between food that is enjoyed and food that is endured. Lacking salt has been associated throughout the highlanders' history with times of exile and deprivation. It is the one essential commodity that cannot be foraged, hunted or made oneself. There must be other people around to trade for it. Not having salt seemed almost a shorthand for loneliness.

The food was bland. Life was bland. Every day, Moun woke up and saw the same people, who spent their days in much the same way he did. There was nothing to do but occupy himself with the business of survival—the daily chores of scavenging and hunting so that he could eat today, and tending to his crops so that he could eat in the future. A war was still raging outside, he believed, and it was not safe to travel far beyond the bounds of the campsite. And even if he had wanted to, even if he had been willing to risk his safety for a glimpse of life outside the camp, he could not do it. He was a Khmer Rouge soldier, and leaving the camp would count as desertion. Moun's life was still not his own.

One day, Moun received word of an execution: three young men apprehended and killed for allegedly plotting to run away. Someone with knowledge of their plans betrayed them. Soldiers waited until the suspects came back from digging cassava, then shot them all. Huon, Moun's brother, was among them.

Decades later, Moun's voice turned bitter when he spoke of his brother's death. "My brother was a good person," Moun said sadly. "Why did they kill him?" He speculated that he was killed out of jealousy. Huon had a good stockpile of food. The senselessness of it pained him.

Huon's death left Moun in a cold and lonely place—fearful of those he was fighting against, distrustful of those he was fighting for. His brother's murder also taught Moun something else: If he ever needed to run away, there could be no hesitation. He would not tell anyone he was going and he would not look back. If he was going to run, he would have to do it well, and make sure that no one ever, ever found him.

Not long after Huon's murder, Moun was called to a meeting with two young women and a young man. He was directed to a petite woman of about 18, with small eyes and an upturned nose. Like every other woman at camp, she wore her black hair bobbed at her chin in the style the Khmer Rouge required of women. Her name was Ath. They'd never met. He found her in no way attractive. This was their wedding day.

Over the years, the Khmer Rouge forcibly married some 250,000[4] couples. These newlywed strangers were ordered to sleep together after their marriages in so-called "love houses." Those who resisted risked torture and execution. Many of these marriages splintered as soon as the parties were out of Khmer Rouge control. Some women viewed the men they were forced to call their husbands as rapists, from whom they escaped at the first opportunity.

Others, however, forged from these grim beginnings a bond of mutual support. With traditional family and social bonds stripped away, these couples had only each another to rely upon. After years of jointly navigating children, hunger and loss, the members of these successful marriages

---

[4] Immigration and Refugee Board of Canada, *Cambodia: Forced marriages; whether forced marriage is currently practised; protection available from the government; consequences for a woman who refuses a forced marriage*, 9 December 2003, KHM42219.FE , available at: http://www.unhcr.org/refworld/docid/403dd1fd8.html [accessed 12 March 2010]

developed true feelings for one another. "The love started for the woman first," explained another man married at O'Chong. "She had been living alone, and she was a female, so she had to have a man to help her, in her tradition. That's why the man starts to have feelings for her, to feel sympathy for her in his heart."

A wedding in their home villages would have been a days-long affair of drinking, music and feasting. Ath's mother would have encouraged her to court many young men before choosing the one she wanted. This ceremony was no more than a public reading of the names of the new couples being joined that day. This woman to that man. Ting Ath to Ly Kamoun. They stood, raised their fists in the air, shouted a slogan in praise of the failed revolution, and that was that.

For the first two or three years, Moun resented the marriage. His feelings changed after the birth of their first child, a girl who arrived in the world slick, red and howling, like a monkey with none of its fur. She needed him, in a way that he had never been needed before, and Ath did as well. "If I love this baby, then I have to love the mother too," he later explained. She was first of seven children that followed over the next twenty-one years.

For what it's worth, Ath thought he was good-looking from the start.

In 1989, Moun was still completely ignorant of life outside the forest. Though he believed he was a soldier on active duty, the war Moun thought he was fighting had been over for ten years, with the Vietnamese occupying Cambodia largely peacefully. The Khmer Rouge controlled only limited territory in the northwestern and northeastern parts of the country, living off food grown by conscripts and civilian semi-hostages like those at O'Chong.

The Vietnamese army and local Cambodian troops made frequent incursions to Khmer Rouge–controlled areas in an attempt to liberate these populations.and weaken the Khmer Rouge by removing their food supply. Though they may have looked like welcome rescue missions to an outsider, the raids were terrifying for those at the receiving end. They didn't know why men with guns were coming for them. They had no information about the state of the country outside the forest, or tools to distinguish fact from rumor and lies. When soldiers stormed their settlements, ostensibly to bring the highlanders home, many of them just burrowed deeper into the forest, the one place that could always be counted on.

In 1989, they came for the people at O'Chong. Time and trauma wreak havoc on memory, and survivors' recollections of the raid are fractured and contradictory. Some people remembered guns and violence; others said the decision to leave the camp was a quieter, less dramatic affair.

Moun and his compatriots could not recall in detail the moment of their leaving or how they arrived at the decision to flee into the surrounding forests. They were six young families, carrying between them a few cooking pots, machetes, axes, rice, a handful of seeds, baskets, and two guns.

The men led the way, hacking brush from their path with swift, powerful thwacks of their machetes. The children traveled in slings against their mothers or on their fathers' backs. Days of walking turned into weeks. The eldest children were about 6; the youngest were babies who nursed as their mothers walked. The landscape inched past. The going was slow. The children in arms grew tired and slept, and the adults walked. They had no destination, no route or map to follow. It was not a part of the forest they recognized. They were simply moving away from the ugliness behind them.

After a month, they came to an area with a tall shading tree canopy overhead, diffusing the intensity of the sun and rain. A secondary layer of shorter trees grew beneath those and would provide wood for shelter. It was remote enough that no one would see the smoke from their cooking fires or hear the explosive sound of their burning bamboo. There was lots of good bamboo, the big thick round kind that grows best on land that has previously been used for farming, and they were heartened to know that this place had supported people before. They built six small houses where parents and children slept side by side at night. The adults were all in their twenties and thirties, with no one in the world to consult but one another.

None of them knew that the camp behind them was the last contact some would have with society for the next fifteen years. For some of them, it was the last village they would ever know.

Their first year in the forest was lean as they waited for the first harvest of rice, chilis and garlic. In the meantime, they trapped fish and critters for protein and scavenged for tubers and edible leaves. The men used their bullets judiciously for bigger game like gibbons. It was a fertile area with no competition for resources. To compensate for the chill at night in the cool dry months, Ath made a blanket from long strips of tree bark soaked and pounded until it was pliable, then stitched together with a long piece of thin vine. She and Moun slept under the scratchy brown blanket at night. Slowly all of their disintegrating Khmer Rouge–issued clothing was replaced by loincloths from this tree bark material. It wasn't the most comfortable cloth in the world, but it worked.

They ended their evenings around a fire, a speck of light piercing a vast emptiness. Their low voices joined the gibbon calls and nighttime forest rustlings as they sat together reviewing the day, laughing and telling stories. They men took turns patrolling the area around their campsite, checking for unfamiliar footprints or unexplained broken grass. They weren't afraid all the time. As they grew comfortable with this new life, fear and tension were replaced largely by boredom, the comforting but mundane repetition of their daily acts of survival.

The soil gave back in abundance everything they put into it. Their rice grew easily. Heaps of the dried white stuff sat in each family's bamboo house. They had so much that each family built a tiny storage shed where they piled the surplus in undulating white hills, alongside seeds carefully saved from each crop. They ate all they needed to replenish the thousands of calories their exhausting daily labors consumed. There was even enough left over to ferment for sweet, potent wine. The only thing they lacked were vessels to make it in, until someone stumbled across an old highlander cemetery left over from the land's long-gone inhabitants. When a highlander dies, his family builds a simple shed on top of his grave and fills it with luxuries like gongs, jewelry, and rice wine jars. Moun's clan simply swiped a few, reasoning they'd outlived their usefulness to the spirits. Rice wine made the evenings around the fire all the more enjoyable. A first harvest passed, then another, and as the years went by the camp became a home.

Their first new member arrived just a few months after they arrived at the campsite, and more followed in short order. Every few months brought another baby, delivered with the assistance of one of the women, a self-trained midwife who kneaded the women's bellies vigorously to coax the child out.

New babies depressed Moun. Another child meant another mouth to feed, another person to support. Small children added problems without much benefit. The adults were constantly warning the children not to shout when they played, lest they attract unwanted attention. If they really needed to reinforce the point, they let slip that tigers found disobedient children especially tasty.

And like at O'Chong, here was still no salt, an absence that only underscored the monotonous nature of forest life. Having never tasted seasoned food, Moun's children didn't know what they were missing. But he did. He grew up with feasts to mark the important occasions in a village's life—the start of the rice harvest, the annual offering to the spirit, the joining of two families in a wedding, the loss of a member to death. He remembered roasted buffalo dripping with pepper- and garlic-infused juices, luscious fruits plucked from the trees, and jars and jars of sweet rice wine. And he remembered the voices laughing with intoxication, the rhythm of dancing feet against the earth as gongs played into the night.

Moun didn't need any more reminders of how alone they were and how likely it was they would die out there. He was reminded with every bite of food he scooped up with his fingers, consumed for no other reason than to keep himself alive, no other celebration but the survival of one more day. They were surviving, yes, but it was not really living. He didn't have a real home, he had no guarantee that he would ever see home again, and as if he needed any further proof of this, he didn't have any damn salt.

III

I had been in Ratanakiri for a few months interviewing Moun and the other returnees when I met Dr. Ian Baird, a social geographer who has worked extensively with the highlander communities scattered across the Laos-Cambodia border. Villagers he'd met on his research trips had told him about the hideaways years before the media ever caught up to them, Ian said, or indeed before they'd even come out of the forest.

Locals had long whispered of a group of Khmer Rouge holdouts living in the forest. Their location and dates matched those of Moun's group. They were armed, people said, and ready to kill anyone who came across them.

In fact, Ian said, there were rumors that they had killed already.

The incident that drew police to their camp and took away some of their number was not a random event. They'd killed people—several people—and they were wanted men.

At once, it all made sense—the fleeting references to an arrest, the sudden changes in their number, their unwillingness to be pinned down on certain parts of their chronology. I replayed our meetings in my mind yet could not reconcile this story of violence with Moun, the unassuming, gentle man who had welcomed me in his home.

Ian was leaving the next day for a five-day research trek through some of the villages where he'd first heard these reports, and eagerly I accepted the invitation to go. The truth seemed closer than ever.

Sound came before light in the early mornings: the crackling of sticks and dry brush under dogs' paws or chicken claws, the snuffling of pigs, the crow of an impertinent rooster. After waking at sunrise at the home of one of Ian's many friends, we packed our mosquito nets and walked for hours through dry lowland forest dotted with farms in various states of regrowth and messy clusters of bamboo. We passed one small village where half a dozen men and women were helping a neighbor castrate a boar. Those pinning the animal down called out greetings as we passed. The man with the cleaver lifted his bloodied hand in a friendly gesture of hello. A testicle lay purple and gleaming in the dirt.

We walked to the district capital of Taveng, a town of little more than a few wooden houses, low-slung concrete administrative buildings and a market stall or two lining a straight dirt road. Ian had heard that local authorities in Taveng had tried to find Moun's group in the mid-1990s and bring them out of the forest. Some of the men involved in this operation still lived in town.

We were received at the home of a man named Up Deu, the chief of Taveng district, who was deputy chief in the mid-1990s. One of the most powerful politicians in the region, Up Deu greeted us wearing nothing but a gold watch and a thin red-and-white checkered krama knotted about his hips. He offered us a seat on the shaded portico of his wooden home. Staring down from the walls were three larger-than-life-size portraits of Hun Sen, Chea Sim and Heng Samrin, the three men who'd governed Cambodia since their installation by the Vietnamese in the 1980s. We were joined by a short and feisty man named Mo Shun, who was the district police chief at the time of the raid, plus a younger man who was also a former soldier.

As the tinkling sounds of music from a nearby wedding wafted through the house, the three men told the following story. Later, Moun and others confirmed the men's report and added details of their own. This is what happened, as reconstructed from the archives of their memory.

Every day, people prowl the forests overlapping Indochina's jigsaw-like borders in search of items to sell. The land where Cambodia, Laos and Vietnam come together is a treasure trove of nature's rarities: trees whose carved and heavily varnished trunks furnish the finer living rooms of Shanghai and Ho Chi Minh City; animals whose scales, skin, penises and blood are sought after in well-appointed medicine cabinets from South Korea to San Francisco. It isn't legal to carry most of these things away, but the forest is so big and the laws so poorly enforced that the local and international conventions against poaching or scavenging or whatever you want to call it are often ignored, even by the people meant to be enforcing them. Virachey National Park is just slightly bigger than Yosemite National Park.. If you want to smuggle out a few key animal organs, it is unlikely that anyone will stop you.

Virachey's remote location means that it still holds plentiful stores of goods extinct in more easily accessible areas. As such, the park attracts a certain type of scavenger: one with a particularly strong taste for adventure or money, and a well-honed instinct for finding things that others overlook. They are usually young and male.

In mid-1994, four such men entered the forest in search of *aquilaria agallocha*, also known as eaglewood, one of the rarest and most prized woods in the world. Scattered across the forests of Southeast Asia and northern India, eaglewood trees produce delicate, spring-green blossoms and a resin with a rich, earthy scent. In Japan and the Middle East the resin is used to produce luxurious incense and oils. It's also believed to possess medicinal properties ranging from the spiritually cleansing to the aphrodisiac. An ounce of the highest-quality eaglewood resin favored by Japanese connoisseurs has sold at times for roughly the equivalent of an ounce of gold.

Greed and desperation sometimes trump common sense. Eager scavengers have ravaged the forests in search of eaglewood; rookies who don't recognize the rotting portion of a tree where the resin forms will chop healthy trees to bits in a fruitless bid to find it. These four scavengers, all men from Vietnam, were searching for a rare and well-hidden prize. They stumbled instead across a well-hidden people.

It isn't clear if one of the Vietnamese met Moun's group alone and brought his friends back later, or if the four encountered them all at once. The four men are all lost now in one way or another; it's impossible to know what they saw. What seems certain is that when the scavengers met the forest people, not another soul in the world knew the hideaways were out there—not their families, not their enemies, not the Khmer Rouge, not the police.

The meeting was a surprise to both sides. The scavengers carried supplies in satchels slung over their shoulders—axes, machetes, hammocks. They had been walking for days, and they were hungry. Moun and the other families had been living in the forest for five years. They were four couples, a single woman, two widows and more than a dozen children among them. Those who wore any clothing at all were clad in only scraps of tree bark cloth. They had, however, managed to bank enormous stockpiles of rice that looked mouthwateringly tempting to the famished travelers.

The relationship wouldn't have lasted forever. The scavengers would have moved on, probably in just a few days. They would have sought out a different corner of the forest in search of their precious wood. If they ever mentioned the forest people's existence, it would probably have been only anecdotally, a story swapped with men of similar occupation while reflecting on the oddities of the trade.

By the time the ill-fated entanglement of these two parties was over, three men would be dead. A mother would lose her children. The lost tribe would turn from refugees to fugitives, retreating even further into the forest.

Of course, no one knew that yet. The scavengers just knew that they were hungry. And as painfully simple as it seems in hindsight, the highlanders just wanted some salt.

At the time they met the scavengers, the group had had no contact with another human for five years, not since fleeing O'Chong. Life had grown more difficult with the passage of time. One of the men contracted a disease known in Khmer as *chuul chkuet*—literally, the "crazy sickness," most likely rabies. He died four months later, leaving his wife Thim pregnant with their sixth child.

They had no language in common with the hideaways, but the scavengers were able to communicate that they were hungry, and that they wished to trade salt for rice—a welcome exchange on both sides. The scavengers returned on each of the next two days. The hideaways communicated with the Vietnamese men only through pointing and pantomime, unable to ask any of the questions they so desperately wanted answered. It was impossible to relax with these strangers so close to their home. But the salt was just so good.

After the Vietnamese left one night, Moun and the other men conferred. Despite the benefits of the relationship, despite the fact that the scavengers hadn't done anything to threaten them, their paranoia was deeply entrenched. Cambodia had been at war for the majority of Moun's life. Violence was his default expectation.

What were they doing out there? Who were they working for? These men were young and strong, just the way a soldier would be. The Khmer Rouge drilled into their heads the presence of spies, infiltrators—who was to say that these benign-seeming men weren't agents for someone else? And they were Vietnamese! How could they know that on the next visit they wouldn't slit all their throats and slide knives up the children's bellies, eat their livers, take their strength—or tip off someone who would?

Moun was not by nature a bloodthirsty man, nor were the men who had become his comrades and family. They took no pleasure in death. But this was war, and in war, the rules are different. They were not fighting for a side—they'd dropped out of that game five years ago, the day they left O'Chong and the Khmer Rouge behind. They were fighting for their own survival. Since the Khmer Rouge took him away from his village, leaving his childhood dead in the mud in Kalai, Moun had been fighting death with everything he had. In his own quiet way, every march he finished, every punishment endured was a protest on behalf of his right to live. They would not risk all they had worked for. The scavengers had to die.

The plan was simple. When the scavengers next returned to the campsite, the highlanders invited them for a drink of their sweet, potent homemade rice wine. As their watchful hosts refilled the wine jar, each man in turn took long pulls from the bamboo straw protruding from the lid. Did they notice anything unusual, these young men, or feel any discomfort as the straw was passed around? Did they ever trust these strange people in the forest? Maybe they felt a vague and unsettling premonition; maybe they sensed nothing but the pleasurably warm sensation of the alcohol taking effect, slowing their reactions, slackening their muscles, unfocusing their vision. Soon, all of them were drunk.

The forest people worked quickly. They pushed the young men's faces against the earth, and bound their hands with thread-thin vines as strong as nylon ropes. Then they shot them. It is not possible to kill four men at the same time with two guns. Their victims had at least a few moments to understand, in a flash of sickening terror, what their fate would be.

And there was time for one wounded man to wrench himself away from his captors' grasp and run into the darkness. They did not chase him. They were out of bullets anyway.

They stripped the dead men of their clothing, tossing their trousers and satchels aside.

Using heavy sticks as shovels, they dug shallow graves at the edges of camp and heaved three naked corpses inside. They shoveled dirt over the men's faces, these men whose names they never knew, and the bodies disappeared into the earth.

The men in Taveng who told us the story seemed uninterested in the fate of the nearly murdered man, who walked for days through the forest before reaching the district town and reporting the group to police. They mentioned that he was wounded but they didn't note how. He seemed to be an irrelevant detail. Cambodia is famously xenophobic toward its larger and more powerful neighbor to the east. The murders of a few Vietnamese traipsing illegally around their forests didn't rouse much sympathy in Ratanakiri.

Authorities were far more concerned about his assailants. The police understood from the scavenger's description that the people who shot him were one of the scattered groups of Khmer Rouge holdouts rumored to still be hiding in Ratanakiri's forests. During the Vietnamese occupation and the years immediately following it, government soldiers often found groups of frightened highlanders hiding among the trees. Usually these were people who fought for or had been rounded up by the Khmer Rouge, with varying degrees of consent on the highlanders' part. It had been years since the last of those groups was found, however. Authorities didn't think anyone was still living there. As they had done in the past, the police decided to send a team into the forest to tell the hideaways that the war was over and bring them back to their villages.

When Ian asked a local police officer later if he had been part of the group that went to go "catch" the hideaways, the man corrected him. "No," the officer said, taking issue with the verb and its ring of criminality. "We went to go bring them back down." It was an important distinction. No punishment awaited them. Many of the soldiers on these expeditions to flush out Khmer Rouge holdouts sympathized with the people they were trying to apprehend. They had also spent years marching at the orders of one army or another, living in wretched camps, constantly afraid for themselves and their families. They understood how frightened these people were, and looked at these missions as a chance to help people much like themselves.

This wasn't always easy. A soldier had his foot blown off in 1985 after stepping on a mine that one of the groups planted in retreat. He lived, but the story was a powerful reminder that the people in the jungle were still very much at war, even if the rest of the country had moved on.

Ironically, the men telling me the story surmised, the Vietnamese would probably never have disclosed the group's hiding place if they had lived. The only reason police ever found them was because of the wounded man's report.

"If those Vietnamese hadn't been up there to look for eaglewood, and [the wounded man] hadn't taken us up there, we would never have found them," Mo Shun said. "We had no idea."

It took a month to round up a few dozen district and provincial soldiers for the expedition. The team spent five days hiking to the camp. There was no clear path through the heavy vegetation, and the soldiers were frequently forced to backtrack as they picked their way through. Most of them were farmers themselves, and as they hiked they admired the quality of the land, with its plethora of big trees and good bamboo.

On the fifth day, sensing that they were closing in, the force sent a few scouts ahead to check out the terrain. At around 9 o'clock in the morning, the scouts came across an animal trap, a clear sign that humans were living nearby. As the soldiers examined the trap, one of them looked up. Watching them through the trees was a square-jawed man with a young boy: Luong and his son Mao. Both sides immediately understood that a chase was on. Luong and Mao turned and ran into the forest, making their way back to the camp as fast as they could to warn the others.

The soldiers considered their options. They knew they were approaching a very frightened group of people who were armed and prepared to kill (they would have been relieved to know that the group spent their last bullets on the scavengers). There could be guns, mines or homemade traps waiting for them. The soldiers were also armed, but scared and hoping to avoid a firefight. They wanted to ensure that none of their moves would prompt the forest people to fire first. As he told the story in Taveng, Mo Shun pointed his fingers like a gun barrel and with comedic flair pantomimed a soldier creeping nervously on patrol, prompting peals of laughter from the other men on the portico.

The scene at the camp was pandemonium. They threw pots, machetes, and whatever else they could carry into back-baskets laden until the woven straps dug into their bare shoulders. There was too much rice to carry away all at once and no time to do more than grab a few handfuls for the next meal. Children old enough to walk were told to run. Some women tied their littlest ones to their backs with slings and carried their baskets in front. Thim, the widow, was seven months pregnant. She loaded a basket on her back, balanced an infant on her hip, grabbed her next-smallest daughter by the hand and waddled awkwardly out of camp with the others.

For the first one hundred yards the fugitives cut no vegetation from their path, taking the scratches and slashes of the dense foliage to throw their pursuers off their trail. After a safe distance, the men began slicing the branches with swift swings of their machetes so that the rest could pass more easily. With the forest obscuring the sounds behind them, they were soon convinced that they were safe.

Behind them, the soldiers crept ahead quietly in groups of ten, spaced five meters apart. At about 11:30 in the morning, more than two hours after they saw Luong and Mao, they reached the hastily abandoned camp. Cautiously the soldiers poked their guns around. They called out in Khmer and two different indigenous tongues. Silence.

In the clearing were six small wooden houses, each with a generous store of rice inside. A narrow path led to a rice field with six small barns, each filled with even bigger heaps of rice. The farmer-soldiers were impressed. They were also hungry. It was lunchtime, and Cambodians allow very few things—even a police pursuit—to interfere with lunch. They built a fire and helped themselves to the grain.

After the meal, the search began again. The forest was so dense that they couldn't see anyone or anything except the trees and the men directly around them. The trail led over three small mountains, and at the top of the last one the soldiers looked down and saw the smoke of a cooking fire below. The forest people had misjudged their lead and stopped for lunch too.

At the sound of the soldiers closing in, the families scattered. None of them thought—or were willing—to help those who couldn't go as fast.

Thim lagged behind. She was barefoot, pregnant, carrying a heavy basket of supplies on her back and herding five terrified children through a forest so dense she couldn't see beyond the next tree. After more than a mile of this, she knew she had no chance. As she heard the soldiers approaching behind, and saw the people she had lived with as family disappear into the trees ahead, Thim made a decision.

"Run!" she screamed to her older children. There was no time to say goodbye. Weeping and clutching her smallest two, she watched her two older boys and her skinny little daughter disappear with the rest of the party into the forest. Then she prepared to die.

The soldiers fired their guns into the air and shouted at her to lie down. Thim's daughter dropped her hand and prostrated, but with her big belly Thim could only stand. She was sobbing. Another woman from the group, a widow named Pheap, was caught too. The rest of the children were nowhere to be seen. A soldier ran up to Thim and grabbed the basket on her back, firmly but not violently, and the women began to plead for their lives.

Both women were naked from the waist up. Around their hips were fastened makeshift skirts fashioned from the Vietnamese scavengers' bags. The soldiers were moved by their obvious terror. There was no sign of anyone besides the shivering women and two small children in front of them. The soldiers were not rough. They explained as

103

best they could that they were not there to punish or hurt them. Warily, Pheap called out to her other children. To the soldiers' surprise, six tiny, dirty faces framed by matted hair peeked out from under logs, between bamboo stalks, under clumps of leaves.

Over several days, the soldiers, women and children slowly walked back to Taveng. At one of the campsites the men purchased a cow from a local villager and slaughtered it for meat. That night the soldiers danced around the campfire to entertain themselves. Thim sat silently and watched the flames.

Meanwhile, once convinced that the soldiers were gone, Moun and the other men crept back to the old campsite to get their rice, seeds and any crops they could salvage. They were certain that Thim, Pheap and the children were dead, and they couldn't risk the rest of their lives by staying in a compromised area. They needed all the provisions they could possibly carry. A very long journey lay ahead.

The authorities tried one more time to find the forest people. In December 1994, a few weeks after the initial raid, a smaller group of about fifteen soldiers went back to the place where the scavengers died. The houses and the rice barns stood empty. The soldiers set the buildings aflame. They nailed to a tree a sign in Khmer that read, "Don't be afraid, you can come back." But the hideaways couldn't read, and they never did come back, anyway.

A few days after hearing this story, Ian and I sat on the rough hewn benches beneath the eaves of Moun's stilt home and talked to Moun for the first and only time about the killings. Ath tended a fire and listened without comment as a handful of children snuggled against each other on the bench next to their father. As we spoke, dusk turned into night. The village beyond the campfire was an opaque black. The fire and my flashlight illuminated the contours of Moun's face, red on one side, ghostly white on the other.

Clearly and calmly he confirmed everything the police told us. Ian joked that the authorities thought they'd eaten the corpses; Moun laughed. "No," he said. "We buried them." He didn't seem disturbed by the memories or the questions. They'd killed the unarmed men, he said, because they feared that the scavengers would eventually turn and kill them or would report them to someone else who would.

There was no hesitation or conflict in his voice; he wore the same calm, half-smiling expression as when we'd talked about farming or the children. To Moun, the decision to kill was a logical one, a calculated risk of war. There were many decisions from that time that he regretted, but killing the scavengers was not one of them. Had they lived, the young men could have endangered the family; dead, they were a neutralized threat. *To keep you is no value, to kill you is no loss.* Moun may have abandoned the Khmer Rouge when he fled O'Chong in 1989, but he never stopped fighting.

I asked Moun if it was harder to live in the forest after they shot the men. Was he worried that he'd be punished for the murders? Did it change anything? He shook his head dismissively.

"No," he said. "We were scared before, and we were scared after."

"Who did it?" I asked. "Who pulled the trigger?"

"That's not an appropriate question," Ian replied, looking at me sharply. "You can't assign culpability to a single person like that." To pull one person out of the web of collective responsibility, he argued, would leave him exposed. They made the decision together; like the firing squads who don't know which gun contains the fatal bullet, the shared burden of responsibility protected them all. *When all are guilty, nobody is,*[5] Hannah Arendt wrote. Moun may have fired a deadly shot into the back of a young man's skull, or he may have stood by as someone else did. The truth changes nothing.

There was one troubling unresolved issue about Moun's story, and that was the matter of Thim—the captured pregnant woman—and her children. A year after the arrests, all of those who

---

[5] Hannah Arendt, "Collective Responsibility," *Responsibility and Judgment* (Random House: 2003), 147.

had run away into the forest were still alive—
except for two. The only two people who did not
survive that first year were Thim's young sons.
(She reunited with her daughter in 2004.)

The men had insisted they'd treated those
children like their own. The boys called them
"uncle," they told me. They were all hungry in that
difficult first year after the murders, after they'd
abandoned their crops at a former campsite and
awaited the first harvest at a new one. They were
all skin and bones, they said, all near starvation. But
the fact remained that out of all the hungry people
in that camp, of all the malnourished children, the
only ones who died were the ones who did not have
a parent to watch out for them. I could imagine the
kind of excruciating choices a parent would have to
make given too little food and too many mouths to
feed, the terrible battle between conscience and
love. It was a time when I desperately wished I had
found a way to talk to the women, alone. I think
mothers would have told a very different story.

Months earlier, just after that day at Moun's
house when he and the other men mentioned the

arrests, we traveled together to visit Thim, the mother of those lost boys. We gathered on the floor of her home in Nhang village. There was no talk of murder. They said only that they had been arrested, but seemed to stop hearing the translator whenever we asked why.

Thim spoke with a kind expression on her face, her legs tucked to the side, her hands resting gently in the folds of a diamond-print sarong. She shared the house with a single female relative who had pasted magazine shots of swooning Khmer couples to the bamboo wall above her sleeping mat. More than a dozen curious women and children from the village settled in to listen.

By the time she reached the district town after her arrest, Thim said, she understood two things: she wasn't going to die, and she was never going to see her children again. The highlanders living in the village where the soldiers brought her were caring, gracious hosts. Once back in civilization she and the other captured woman became keenly embarrassed by their nakedness, and a local girl gave them some of her own skirts and blouses. There was salt, which the heavily pregnant Thim at first took only sparingly because she was afraid she would bloat. She soon delivered a healthy child. But an ache entered her body that would never go away.

She'd hoped Luong would watch out for her children. He was from the same ethnic group, the Tampuon, and like her children spoke Tampuon as a first language. As one of the oldest men, Luong exuded a fatherly warmth. "I still had a little bit of a dream that my children could live with him," she said quietly as she recounted the story almost fifteen years later.

As the years passed she would sometimes stop to watch other children the same ages as her missing ones. She imagined what her children would look like, what kind of people they might be. "Every time I dreamed," she said, "I thought about my other children."

Word of the forest people's return in 2004 reached Thim in Nhang just days after the group arrived in Banlung. Thim tried in vain to find a motorbike taxi to drive her through the night on the unlit roads to the capital, but had to settle for a driver willing to leave at the first light of the next day. She arrived in Banlung with overinflated hopes, searching for three faces she expected to recognize immediately.

At the sight of her daughter she broke down in tears. Her daughter was only a small girl when they parted; now, she was a young woman, though thin and sickly from her ordeal. But the girl did not recognize her. She looked at her mother like she was a stranger. Then Thim looked for her boys, and when she did not see them, she wept with the pain of losing them all over again.

On the floor of Thim's home, fourteen years later, her kind face stayed neutral when Moun swore emphatically that he had done all he could to take care of her children, but that nothing could be done to prevent their deaths. As he spoke, Thim's daughter appeared in the doorway of the hut. Now 20 years old, she was a lovely, graceful young woman, with a glossy black ponytail, full cheeks and a radiant smile. Thim looked at her adult daughter as a mother does a newborn child.

I asked Thim about her siblings, and if their lives had been as difficult as hers. She had one brother, she replied, a soldier who was decommissioned from the army and sent home to live in their village after getting his legs blown off.

She sighed. "He was lucky," she said.

Ten years passed between the time that Moun and his family fled the police and the day they emerged from the forest in November 2004. They established a pattern they followed for a decade—set up camp, live two or three years until an unfamiliar footprint or freshly cut branch appeared, then pack up their things and move even deeper into the forest. In fifteen years of wandering, they walked across the international border from Cambodia to Laos, over steep hills and dense jungle where tigers still roamed.

Once they established a camp and planted their crops, there was not much to do but hunt, drink rice wine and make children. By their late teens the oldest of their children began to pair off. In the lack of formal ceremony, their simple forest weddings mirrored their parents' Khmer Rouge–era ones. "We asked the girl, 'Do you want to love this boy for life?' We asked the boy, 'Will you love this girl for life?'" Chakov told me. "If the answer is yes, we started drinking."

But there was a crucial difference. These young people chose each other, albeit from a very small sample. Their parents brought them up in the forest precisely to allow them the experience they had been denied.

During these years, they were completely off the world's radar—no evidence exists to verify how they spent this time. Once I found out about the murders, I realized there was no telling what else they might be concealing. Some secrets remain in the forest; they will die with the people who keep them.

The returnees were never able to clearly articulate why they decided to make contact with the world after a decade in isolation. The men said they simply grew tired of forest life, that their health and morale were failing. The death of their eldest male companion seemed to stoke anxieties among the surviving adults that they too might die without ever seeing their ancestral homes again. In contrast to the years spent justifying the choice to stay hidden, they now began to look for indications that it was safe to come out.

Their last move brought them to a location within a day's walk of a highlander village in southern Laos. The proximity to human settlement may be the reason their health took a turn for the worst. Disease vectors like mosquitoes can only travel so far, and the isolated locations of their previous camps inoculated them from diseases like malaria and cholera. As they approached society, however, their unchallenged immune systems came under attack. Luong's wife took ill with fever, chills and a splitting headache—the early signs of malaria. They needed help.

At this point it had been roughly fifteen years since they had seen direct evidence of gunfire, soldiers or other signs that the nation was still at war. They were ready to consider the possibility that Cambodia had at least achieved some kind of peace. It's also possible that the story is far more complicated than they are willing to admit, and that their decision was shaped by other reasons they prefer not to reveal.

In early November 2004, two of the group's young men were fishing at the nearby stream when they overheard unfamiliar voices speaking Brao, a highlander language similar to Kreung. Before the young men could hide themselves, the fishermen noticed them and beckoned them to come closer.

"Who are you?" asked one of the Brao fishermen, unused to seeing a new face at this particular fishing spot.

It was the first time either of the young men had ever been asked that question—in fact, it was the first time they had ever spoken to anyone outside of their families. They answered as simply as they could.

"We are forest people," one of the young men replied. "We live in the forest."

Overwhelmed by curiosity and reassured by the assumption that the men were of their same ethnic background, the young men invited the four fishermen to accompany them to their camp. As far as anyone of the surviving forest people is willing to admit, this was their first encounter with an outsider in ten years, since shooting the Vietnamese scavengers.

The young men took the fishermen to Luong, who was then the oldest surviving male among them and thus, at the age of about 40, their de facto elder. It was about 3 o'clock in the afternoon—he remembered this from the position of the sun—when Luong looked up from his small plot of rice crops and saw the young men approaching in the company of strangers.

"At first I was frightened," Luong told me later. "I am the oldest man in the group, and so I felt responsible for our people. I worried that they had weapons or grenades. I don't know them, I can't see what they have. I was afraid at that time that they would kill us if they had any weapons. Our first concern was our life."

He was not angry at the young men for violating the sanctuary of their camp. He and Moun both said later that the fishermen's shared ethnic background was key to the decision to trust them. If other highlander men were spending their days fishing rather than fighting, then perhaps it was a sign that peace had returned. Luong must have known that these men represented as good a chance as any at finding a way home.

"The first thing they said was, 'Is this your field?'" Luong recalled. "And I said, 'Yes, this is our field, this is where we grow our rice. This is where we have been living. We have been moving from place to place, trying to connect to another community, hoping to meet somebody.' And they said, Yes, okay. And then we invited them to drink." The fishermen accepted, unaware of the fate of the forest people's last guests.

I try to imagine what this bizarre summit must have been like for the parties involved—the campfire casting a dull red glow on shadowed faces, the forest people at once terrified and fascinated by these envoys from the outside world, scrutinizing their every word and movement for clues about life beyond their forested prison. Where even to begin? What to ask first after ten years separated from the world? This meeting could be the beginning of their future or their demise. Whatever the outcome, they were willing to take the risk. Life had finally become more intolerable than fear of the unknown.

The forest people asked where they were, and the fishermen told them that they were in Attapeu, the southernmost province of Laos. As the wine flowed and the night grew deeper, the forest people gathered the courage to ask their most pressing question.

"And then once we were drunk we became very straightforward, and we asked them about Cambodia here, what was the situation," Luong said. "And they told us, 'We do not know if there is tension there or not. But in Laos, there is no war. If you want to go to Laos it's okay because there is no war, no fighting.'"

The forest people had heard all they needed to hear. One of their own people had told them in their own language that they were in a peaceful country. The matter was settled. If Laos was at peace, then in Laos they would stay. If moments ago they were fugitives, now they were asylum seekers.

"Take us back with you to your village," Luong asked.

The fishermen, understandably, were less than enthusiastic about this. Imagine how their strange companions looked to them: the children naked, the adults clad only in strips of tree bark wrapped around their midsections. The forest people allowed that they were "from Cambodia"—they would not mention their former Khmer Rouge affiliation until they were back in Ratanakiri and convinced that their past would not threaten their future. But the fishermen must have sensed that this was not merely a particularly hardy group of migrants.

"Wait ten days," the fishermen told the forest people, "and we'll come back for you then." With that, they left.

Eagerly, the forest people prepared to leave their camp. At that point, their belongings amounted to little more than a few battered pots and a couple of machete blades. They filled fraying baskets with rice, seeds and vegetables, unsure of how long this final journey would take.

Patiently they waited through ten sunsets and sunrises, anxiously counting off each one. Ten days passed, and when the men did not return on the tenth day, or the eleventh or the twelfth, the forest people decided that they'd been stood up.

"Maybe they were frightened because we had too many people in our group, thirty people. We were frightened of them and they also were frightened of us. We scared each other," Luong recalled. "We waited a long time and then we felt like maybe they had cheated us or mistreated us, those four men, so we decided to leave the area before they came back."

The first rays of morning light turned the forest from black to indigo blue as the families set off. There was a long walk ahead of them, and they wanted to get moving before the day became uncomfortably warm. The sky cycled through a vibrant spectrum of red, magenta and orange before settling into pale, colorless light.

It was one of the most difficult journeys undertaken so far. They were herding roughly a dozen children under the age of 12, who marched along with stoicism far beyond their years. Moun's daughter-in-law was immensely pregnant, and with a full basket of rice on her back and a heavy belly in front she could barely keep up. Luong's wife was so weak with malaria that he had to carry her on his back for most of the journey. All of them were barefoot, save for Chakov, who had found an abandoned tire some years before and fashioned himself a pair of sturdy and much-treasured sandals from the thick rubber tread.

The men walked in front, slashing brush out of their way. Their calloused feet barely registered the texture of the sandy soil. They walked in silence. The only sounds they added to noises of the forest were the occasional mewing of a hungry baby, quickly silenced with a breast, and the rustle, swish and *thwack* of the men clearing the path ahead.

Moun was an experienced tracker. Daily he'd searched the haystack of the forest for needle-thin clues of human contact. So after a full day of walking, he knew even before they reached the worn footpath in the soil that people were nearby. He motioned and the column came to a halt. They dropped their baskets in a grove surrounded by sheltering trees. The women squatted and prepared dinner.

The next morning, Moun and Luong went on to explore ahead. They moved silently, following the footpath in the grass so as not to leave suspicious new prints. Both men had a sense of where the trail was leading. Highlanders make their farms at least a few hundred yards away from their villages—Moun and Luong had kept up the practice in the forest—and the traffic between home and field tended to wear paths just like the one they were following.

Through a break in the trees Moun spied a small cluster of houses. The men paused, and gazed upon the village as though peering onto another world.

Moun and Luong had arrived at Chung Hieng, a tiny settlement of seven to ten highlander families in southern Laos. The houses were empty. It was rice harvest season, and everyone was out gathering the season's crops. Chickens pecked about the dusty ground. Pigs snortled in the distance. Dust-stained T-shirts and faded cotton sarongs hung on pegs protruding from the tiny stilt houses.

Wordlessly, the men moved between houses snatching all the clothes they could carry. Chung Hieng's residents owned little besides what they were wearing at the fields, but Moun was able to grab a few well-worn garments. As they scuttled between the houses, a golden glint caught Moun's eye. He reached out and took hold of something he had never seen before. He looked at the wristwatch's round, appealing face, its hands stretched optimistically toward the perimeter. Moun had stolen things before, but only objects with a purpose, plundered out of necessity. This thing—whatever it was—he took because he wanted it.

The men returned to their camp and distributed the clothes to their families. After a few more days on the edge of the village, they decided to advance closer.

They came upon a villager feeding his pigs. The man looked up and saw them. And then, just like they had always feared, he turned and fled.

"No, don't run! Don't run away!" Luong screamed. But it was too late. Before their painfully slow band of children, malaria patients and pregnant women could make it far, the man returned with a gun and shouted at them to stop.

"We sat down on the road," Luong recalled. "We didn't run back to the forest, because we were worried that they would shoot at us. They had AK-47s, they had B-40 pointed at us, and I decided: I don't care. We don't care anymore. If we die, we die here."

Luong dropped to his knees and put his hands in the air. He spoke to the man in a prisoner of war's vocabulary. "I said, 'We are civilians,'" Luong recounted. "He asked, 'Where are you going?' When he asks this he is pointing the gun at us. We say, 'We want to go to Laos. We want to go to live in Laos because we don't want to live in

Cambodia. And I promise, I will live in Laos, and if I run away, you can kill me and you can kill them all, my whole group.'"

The farmer didn't shoot, of course.

Their hearts pulsing with adrenaline, the men ordered their shaking wives and children to their feet as the man motioned for them to follow. Tear-streaked children clung to their mothers as the families followed him back to the village. As he went to confer with the other men in the settlement, curious women and children gathered around. They were more interested in the bark clothing than their stolen garments.

"Please tell them we'll give back these clothes," Luong said nervously to the farmer.

The man spoke to his fellow villagers, and then turned back to Luong. "Keep them," he said. "They're a gift."

The district town was a day's walk away, the man explained, and a villager had already gone ahead to tell authorities there to prepare their guest house. Military style, with their men in the front and back of the column, three Chung Hieng

125

residents led the forest people down the mountain and northwest toward town. At dusk they reached the Namkong River, and the exhausted families waded across the shallow riverbed.

Once on the other side, the women scavenged for greens to stir over rice cooked in their ancient pot. There was not an electric light for miles and night came on quickly. When the last of the evening sun left the sky, they settled onto the ground and slept.

Before he closed his eyes, Moun looked up at a sky brilliant with stars, the same ones he had looked on as a child, the same ones his family many miles away saw before they slept. It was the last night he would ever spend in the forest.

By the time the sun came up the next morning, word of the forest people had reached Bounnao, a low-level bureaucrat whose job it was to take care of things like unexpected visitors. Bounnao was intrigued. He had heard before of people who lived in the remotest reaches of those hills—*pi tong luen,* or those who live in houses of old, yellow leaves—but it was clear from the Chung Hieng villager's description that there was something different about this crowd. By eight o'clock in the morning, he was piloting the district's twelve-passenger van over the rutted dirt road to the river to pick up the new arrivals.

As the van pulled up to the campsite along the river, the children's eyes—and some of the adults'—grew wide with fear. They had never seen a car before. Gingerly they climbed into the van, which quaked violently over the unpaved roads.

The smoky blue silhouette of the mountains receded into the distance behind them. The women were silent. Moun was apprehensive. The villages they passed looked peaceful; the people who'd greeted them so far seemed genuine. But Moun knew well that looks could be deceiving. Sometimes, people just acted like they had your best interests in mind to serve their own purposes. Sometimes they pretended to be on your side, right up until the moment they killed you.

The district center of Phou Vong was a little town of simple straw and wooden houses with tall trees at the edges and cows and buffaloes munching boredly on the grass outside people's homes. The brightest swaths of color came from the yellow plastic Beerlao crates stacked up against the sides of homes, and from the green-and-yellow bunting celebrating the national beer that hung from nearly every shop and café. The trucks rumbled into town on a stone-clotted red dirt road lined with leaf huts and banana trees. They passed rice paddy fields divided with low stone walls and peopled with farmers in conical hats.

The trucks pulled up to the government guest house next door to the district offices. The tidy two-story wooden building was separated from the road by a lawn pockmarked by a 30-year-old B-52 bomb crater. Large enough to swallow a small truck, the pit was ringed with trees and overgrown by weeds. To Moun and the others, the house looked like a palace.

They arrived around lunchtime. The women of the town prepared for the guests a meal of rice, vegetables and chickens plucked from their own yards and slaughtered for the occasion. They spread out on the floor the woven plastic mats of Southeast Asian villages, whose longevity suggests some sort of ballistic-grade construction. When they motioned for the families to sit down, Luong was horrified.

"I said, 'No! I can't sit on that! It's too nice!'" he recalled with a giggle. After some gentle prodding by his hosts he relented and the rest of the group followed. Then they ate. And ate, and ate, and ate.

This first real, hospitable, properly cooked meal in decades took on almost mythic status in its diners' minds. When Luong described the lunch to me three years later, he insisted that the kettle of rice they were given was approximately the size of the table at which we were seated. When describing the food, Luong's eyes rolled back in his head and he groaned like a person in the grips of religious ecstasy. "Ohh, chnang *na!*" he said in Khmer—It was *so* good! Rice, vegetables, meat they didn't have to hunt themselves—it was overwhelming. And salt. Oh, the salt. It enhanced every bite of the food, an edible, visceral reminder that they were once again back in the world.

For the adults, at least, this was a sublime experience. The children grimaced as they ate. Their food tasted bitter and harsh. What was this stuff?

An audience gathered to watch them while they ate. For the next several days, while they did little besides sit in the guest house and wait to hear of their fate, strangers watched virtually everything they did. All visitors attract some attention in a small town like Phou Vong, but the forest people were, to put it mildly, special. Though their story had not yet gone global, word spread like fire in the dry season of the people who had come from the forest, wild people who dressed in the skin of the trees and didn't know that the war was over. Curious villagers from the other side of the Sekong River arrived by the ferryload. In the surrounding villages and towns, over vegetable stalls in the markets and cups of fragrant mud-thick coffee in the cafés, people asked each other: *Have you seen them? I want to see them. Let's go see them!*

"Everyone was talking, saying, 'Go, go, go!' Everyone was saying, 'Go take a look at these strangers from the jungle,'" said Bounthanh Chanthakhaly, a civil servant and former Pathet Lao revolutionary in Phou Vong. "The boat man made a lot of money off them."

Everyone remarked on their skimpy clothes. The women's bark skirts reached only to mid-thigh, scandalously short by local standards. Also, children as young as 5 or 6 smoked cigarettes right along with their parents, having learned on homegrown tobacco in the forest. Within the first few days of their arrival Bounnao secured money from the local government to purchase two sets of clothes for each person. They also got decent haircuts.

When they arrived at the Phou Vong guest house, people hoping to see half-feral wildmen were let down by the sight of men, women and children in cotton trousers, printed sarongs, button-down blouses and T-shirts. Bounthanh too was a little

131

disappointed to find that the people of the forest looked unimpressively similar to those he already knew. "Oh, it's our people," he remembered thinking. "It's people just like us."

The attention was overwhelming for the new arrivals. "So many people came to see us!" Luong remembered. Before word got back that the forest people weren't all that interesting to look at, men, women and children trooped through the guest house to look. There was even a *barang* among them, a white man, the first that any of them had ever seen. The forest people spoke little to these visitors. What they remembered about their first interactions with other humans was kindness. They ate meat at every meal, chickens or frogs that locals donated from their own supplies. A local doctor came to examine them. A few days after they arrived, Moun's daughter-in-law had a baby girl.

One of the most difficult things for the returnees to get used to was clothing. Nakedness is nothing if not comfortable. They tugged on their new trousers and T-shirts and found the garments chafing and hot. The children complained loudly;

the adults shushed them but secretly felt the same way.

They were more than happy to discard the bark clothes, a symbol of hardship and deprivation. But for the people of Phou Vong, these bark garments were rare and valuable relics, remnants of the hardscrabble times of their ancestors' era. The labor-intensive material was a valuable commodity in the days when cloth was hard to come by. There was once a time when a piece large enough to serve as a blanket for a husband and wife could be traded for one buffalo, the largest and most valuable animal.

Local authorities took one set of clothing away. Soubanh Chanthavong, the high school principal, traded forty shirts from the Red Cross and several other donated items for one of their blankets. When I visited him in Phou Vong, Soubanh agreed to show it to me.

He unrolled it carefully from a nylon tarp onto a table outside his concrete-block home, and I felt a sense of reverence when he lifted it from the shroud. It was about five feet long and eighteen inches wide. Soubanh said that they had had nicer pieces with them, presumably whisked away by the authorities. I had pictured something gray and stiff, like the bark of the tree in my parents' front yard that I stripped and hammered mercilessly with a rock when I was 7 years old, having read about aboriginal peoples who made cloth from trees in just this way. This bark, though, was different. It looked like the hide of an animal. It felt alive. Before I left Soubanh tore off a corner of the blanket and a length of the vine thread and gave it to me. Separated from its parent blanket the remnant feels dry and dead in my hand, like a leaf that has dropped from its tree.

Moun and Luong did not want to go back to Cambodia. Both had long ago decided that if they ever came out of the forest they would happily throw their support behind any party willing to offer them safety and peace. Already they gathered that history did not look fondly on the Khmer Rouge. Privately they decided that it would be best not to mention that part of their life story. (They also omitted, for obvious reasons, any mention of the Vietnamese scavengers.) The story that they gave in Phou Vong was that they were running *from* the Khmer Rouge, that they were afraid of them. They hoped that this would be a more politic narrative.

Their plan failed. After about a week, word came back from the central government in Vientiane that these uninvited migrants needed to go back to where they came from. About nine days after their arrival in Phou Vong, Cambodia's lost tribe prepared to take their leave. They clambered onto the bed of a government truck, a vehicle that some had decided was incredibly exciting and others still found terrifying. Steeling himself for whatever lay ahead, Moun watched as the villagers gathered to see the truck off. There were no hugs, no waving—neither gesture is part of the highlanders' culture. The knot of well-wishers receded into a dusty horizon. Soon he could see them no more.

The cloudy expanse of the Bolaven Plateau rose like a wall on the horizon. The truck rumbled past sparkling white plaster statues of communist revolutionaries, their molded guns raised in solidarity. They passed orange-robed monks on bicycles and schoolgirls in black skirts and white blouses, holding parasols to shield themselves from the sun. In the broad paddy fields partitioned by low dirt walls, farmers bent over their crops, broad straw hats offering small respite from the sun.

There were all kinds of things Moun had never seen before. Glass panes in windows. Satellite dishes. Even the brightly colored photographs and banners affixed to the shops and restaurants were a mystery. In the last society Moun lived in there was no such thing as currency, let alone advertising. The road veered to the right. The trees on the mountains where he had once lived looked like matchsticks.

At the international border, the truck rumbled past the small wooden shack that served as the Lao customs post. The clan disembarked from the cars and crossed the border on foot, passing a colonial-era granite marker carved with the French name: *Cambodge*. The smiling governor of

Ratanakiri province stood before another fleet of trucks that would take them back to the villages where they fervently hoped their families still lived. They knew their parents and siblings believed them dead. They just hoped they weren't too late to tell them the truth.

Once in Cambodia, the landscape turned to scrubland. The trucks braked more often for cows and buffaloes than for other vehicles in the road. Cashew trees dotted the low rolling hills. They crossed O'Pong Moan, the Chicken Egg River. Then the trucks made a wide, lazy U-turn and headed north. For the first time in twenty-five years, Moun could say he was going home.

IV.

Almost two million people died in the four years the Khmer Rouge held Cambodia. Thousands more perished in the deprived years that followed. Many of those who survived the nightmares of the 1970s and 1980s were left with disabling physical and mental injuries. Unlike an amputated limb, however, psychological damage can be handed down to new generations.

Phnom Penh urbanites may insist that they are too focused on the money-making present to bother with the past, but when a construction crew imploded a building without warning several years ago, terrified shopowners and homemakers ran screaming into the streets, dragging their children behind them, to escape the bombs they thought were falling again. Cambodians resent outsiders' implications that they are a nation of shell-shocked survivors, but in 2004 news from police stations around the country made it impossible not to notice how many seemingly pedestrian conflicts escalated into stunning violence: the farmer who beheaded his neighbor with a machete in a dispute over a fence; the disgruntled relative who stormed away from an argument at a wedding and returned to douse the guests with battery acid.

Despite these unfavorable odds, Moun and his family not only survived but thrived. The family's success seemed improbable the first day we met, when the children seemed so ill at ease in their new surroundings and Moun so wary of the new world. Four years later, his success as a farmer, his family's physical health and their close social bonds with the village were impressive by any standard, not only for someone with as tumultuous a past as his.

The anthropologist Jared Diamond once examined[6] several cases of people stranded in extreme isolation: Ishi, the last surviving member of his California Native American tribe; the Japanese holdouts who lived decades in the Philippines after World War II; the mutineers of the H.M.S. *Bounty*, who took to murdering each other upon landing on

---

[6] Diamond, Jared. "Survival in extreme isolation." *Nature* 29 January 1987: 394. Print.

Pitcairn Island. He identified seven key factors that the most successful of these survivors share. His list hewed closely to the social and cultural mores of Ratanakiri's indigenous peoples: *Long familiarity with the environment. Cultural homogeneity. Willingness of individuals to assume new roles for the group's benefit. Non-competitive egos. Shared belief in a righteous purpose.*

Moun's successful landing in the modern world was due in no small part to his village. The family settled in Krala, Ath's home base, a Kreung settlement of tidy stilt wood homes about an hour's drive by motorbike from the provincial capital of Banlung. Land grabs, poverty and a growing desire for material goods that no one had the money to buy threatened the cohesion of many highlander villages in the area, yet Krala held fast as a community. My translator Sotheara and I arrived at the village one day to find every house empty, as men, women and children worked together to fence in the village perimeter so that no unscrupulous land dealer could lay claim to their communally held property. They kept up with some traditional practices—a banana tree fenced off in the village center was home to the resident spirit—while pragmatically adopting modern tools that improved their health and living standards. It was a place that looked after its own.

In contrast, Luong did not fare so well after emerging from the forest. Almost immediately after the family returned to Cambodia, his wife died of malaria. His son got divorced, and the ex-wife— Moun's eldest daughter—took his beloved grandchildren and moved back to her parents in Krala. Bereft of his family, Luong occupied himself by acquiring things, and coveting what he could not have. He was concerned with money—how to get more of it, and the things it could buy. He was in his forties when he was introduced to the concept of currency; now, he had the restlessness of a man always searching for the next get-rich-quick scheme. He wore a faux gold watch dotted with tiny ruby-colored gems. He borrowed money to buy a black motorbike tricked out with fluorescent green spokes, which he used to drive to the local market so that he could spend more money.

Luong lived in a village called Luot, a poorer village than Krala, where trash marred the dirt roads and children had distended bellies. Life was actually easier in the forest, he told me. The only things they really needed that they couldn't scavenge or make themselves were salt and MSG. Life these days was preoccupied with the same struggle for survival, but now the things they needed required cash instead of ingenious sourcing. Still, he coveted the trappings of this new life, and he seemed to resent his disadvantaged past. I asked why he thought he had been singled out for such a different life than his peers, and he looked sad. "I don't know why my life has been like that," he said. "I am a very unlucky man." Then he asked me for money.

The last of Diamond's points stayed with me when I spoke to Moun and the other families: *Shared belief in a righteous purpose.* I knew that conviction in one's actions had brought comfort and strength to pioneers, religious crusaders and soldiers across time and cultures. But Moun's group? What was their campaign? By the time they were out in the forest, they believed in no ideological cause, considered themselves part of no army. When they came out, they were totally ready to pledge allegiance to whatever side was in power, as long as it meant peace. Their only cause was their own survival, the desire to keep themselves and their children alive, day after day, at any cost. "Each day can be broken into two parts," reads a training manual for Australian soldiers trapped in enemy territory, "ensuring that once the sun rises your efforts are directed to staying alive to see it set and vice versa once the sun sets to see it rise."[7] This is the battle Moun waged daily, the one that gave him focus and kept him from losing his mind. They fought to live because they believed that fighting for life was more courageous than surrendering to death. There isn't a more righteous purpose than that.

The Japanese soldier Hiroo Onoda became a global celebrity when he was coaxed out of his hiding spot in the Philippines thirty years after

---

[7] Western Australia Police Academy Command & Land Operations Unit, Aids to Survival, (Western Australia Police Academy: 2002), 16. https://www.uscrow.org/downloads/survival/Aids%20to%20Survival.pdf

Japan's surrender in World War II. President Ferdinand Marcos requested that Onoda come out from the mountains in the tattered remnants of his military uniform. But as they led him down the hill from the jungle to the town, Onoda recalled in his memoir, he would not have minded if a sniper had ended his life right there. Having convinced himself that news of Japanese surrender was enemy propaganda, Onoda was ashamed of his thirty-year fight for a lost cause. His convictions strengthened his will to live, but also trapped him in a prison of his own making. "I constructed an imaginary world that would fit in with the oath I had taken fifteen years earlier,"[8] he said. "[N]ow I alone was returning . . . to a Japan that had lost the war thirty years earlier. Returning to my fatherland for which I had fought until the day before. If there had not been people around, I would have beat my head on the ground and wailed."[9]

Moun had expressed similar shame upon returning to the world and learning that he'd structured his life around lies and misperceptions.

Hiroo Onoda, *No Surrender* (Bluejacket Books: 1999), 126.
Hiroo Onoda, *No Surrender* (Bluejacket Books: 1999), 218-19.

Their path may have been unusually difficult, but the bottom line is that Moun, his wife and his children all survived the Khmer Rouge and its aftermath. Many families did not. His survival tactics were built on false premises, but they worked.

In stories from people who have survived harrowing experiences—shipwrecks, plane crashes, POW camps, isolation—survivors describe a singular moment when their consciousness clears of panic, fear and confusion and acknowledges desire to live. Psychologist Viktor Frankl had his moment on a snowy gray morning as he labored in a trench in a Nazi concentration camp. Through his despair and pain, he wrote, there suddenly came "a victorious 'Yes' in answer to my question of the existence of an ultimate purpose."[10] Such a moment is not the end of the struggles, but rather, as Churchill might say, the end of the beginning. It is the moment when a person pushed to his limits recognizes that he has the choice to stop fighting, and elects—consciously or not—to keep going.

---

[10] Viktor E. Frankl, *Man's Search for Meaning* (Beacon: 2006), 40.

Once this happens—particularly if you then have a lot of time to sit around and think, as Moun and Lt. Onoda had—then you must do things to remind yourself what you are fighting for. That is why Onoda and his comrades made themselves traditional *ozoni* soup on Japanese New Year, and why Moun insisted on carrying a heavy earthenware wine jar on the family's most grueling moves. It is the reason both men stayed fastidiously clean, trimmed their nails and did their best to clothe themselves with what they could find in the jungle.

You have to keep doing the things that make you feel human, to retain as much of your dignity as possible. You must do this because it is likely that the desire to live will push you in directions that you never expected to travel, and will compel you to do things you never, ever imagined you would do. Survival is simply the result of favorable circumstances, a hearty dose of luck and a refusal to quit. "Nothing more than an ordinary life well lived in extreme circumstances," as journalist Laurence Gonzales put it.[11]

Few places have demanded more of ordinary people than Cambodia in the twentieth century. Even now, decades after history says the wars ended, people wake every day to face anew this challenge: to have found out what they were capable of when all they loved was at stake, and to go on living afterward.

Not long ago, I opened a women's magazine in a Manhattan bodega and there, staring back from the glossy page, was Moun.

Sandwiched between articles on floral prints for spring and the dating life of a female pastor was a piece about Kreung love huts, the private bungalows parents build for adolescent daughters to receive their male suitors. The writer had traveled to Krala to report the story. The accompanying photo essay showed Moun's youngest daughter Poeun, then 17, clasping hands

---

[11] Laurence Gonzales, Deep Survival (Norton: 2004), 240.

with one of three current boyfriends. Moun and Ath posed in a separate shot, arms stiffly at their sides. Ath's smile is sweet and cheeky; Moun looks as uncomfortable as any father discussing his daughter's sexuality. "Things are changing. Boys are becoming more arrogant," the article quoted Poeun as saying. "I wish the boys were good so we could continue our old tradition. That would make us so happy." The story made no mention of her unique upbringing. She is a normal teenager now, and to newcomers her family appears no different than any other in Krala.

But save for the occasional serendipitous media appearance, there is no way to keep in regular contact with Moun. He has no phone number. There's no address for the little wooden home in Krala. I could send a telegram to the musty Western Union office in Banlung, but it would sit there unread, as there is no way to tell him that someone in the outside world is thinking of him, and no language he could read if there were. The only way I can know if he is still alive is to fly back to Phnom Penh, take a seat on another crowded minibus, steel my nerves against the drivers' karaoke music, and find my way to Krala again.

Moun seemed to regard our interviews with a sort of patient amusement. I don't think he ever really understood why I was so interested in his story, and frankly I don't think he cared. Moun sees nothing romantic or heroic in his own history. He was young, he was torn away from his community, and he survived thanks to a viciously uncompromising commitment to his family's continued existence. He did only what he had to do to keep his family alive. That community, and not his own biography, is how Moun defines himself. *Life requires other people*, Moun had told me the day we sat in his field, watching the trees crash around us at his will. *You cannot live alone.*

But for all of our conversations, for all our discussions in the shade of his fields or the warmth of his home, Moun remained at his essence an elusive figure, a perpetual man in the woods, offering brief glimpses of himself before retreating into the shadows. I cannot convince myself that he allowed me across the barrier surrounding his most private thoughts. Culture and language play a part, of course, but Moun keeps a high and fortified fence around the years he spent in the forest. A lot of things happened during those years that he has no desire to revisit. For all that he told me, I believe there's far, far more that he left out.

What I learned from Moun, more than anything else, is the difficulty of divining the truth of another human's story. Understanding the whole of a person's life—not just what they did, but why they did it—is like constantly unfolding a puzzle, a Jacob's ladder that spills out in a new direction every time you grasp a different corner.

Moun and his family are the last known holdouts of the Khmer Rouge era to emerge from the jungle. *There can't be anyone else*, insisted the park rangers, historians and others with whom I raised the possibility that others like them are still in the forest. It has been too long; they would have been discovered by now.

Yet there was no reason to believe there was anyone left in the forest in 2004, right up until the day Moun's family appeared. Moun and his comrades insist they saw no one else and say they don't believe there's anyone like them left. They also claimed never to have encountered other people, and that, as I learned, was not true.

In August 2013, nine years after Moun and his family emerged, two men stepped out of the jungle in a remote forested province in central Vietnam. They were a father and son, ages 82 and 41, and members of an indigenous Vietnamese ethnic minority group. When war killed his wife and two other sons, the elder man said, he took his last living child and escaped into the forest, where they lived alone for the next forty years. These "Tarzans of Vietnam," as the *International Herald Tribune* indelicately called them, were photographed with the same tree-bark loincloths, the same blackened pots, the same homemade tools that Moun and his companions described. There's no reason there can't still be others: some who may one day be found, and others who will die in the forest as anonymously as they lived.

If you count his time in the Khmer Rouge labor camp, Moun has only recently passed the point at which the years of his life spent outside the forest exceed the number of years he spent in them. No diaries, logbooks or other records confirm his account of what really happened to his remote secret society. The story of his twenty-five years there survives only in stories, told by him or someone else, and filtered through the distorting lenses of the narrator's memories and agendas. A life reveals itself in artifacts and clues—a sarong missing from a clothesline, a footprint in the soil— and we do the best we can to fill in the rest.

When I think of Moun now, the moment that comes to mind is not the night we spoke of the murders, his fire and my flashlight distorting his face into a garish mask of shadows and light. Instead I recall the sun-drenched afternoon when we gathered in his home with Luong and Chakov to talk about the forest and to reflect on all they had survived together. I wondered aloud if they believed anything else was in store for them, if there were any other unexpected turns their personal histories might take.

Moun closed his eyes wearily and shook his head. "No," he said firmly. "I won't go anywhere else. I will die in this village. We will die together here. No one can force me to go. I'm too tired."

Then he paused, as if to reconsider. "But if everyone else ran, I'd go again."

The End

Acknowledgements

The following people read this manuscript at various stages and contributed wise and insightful edits: Kelly Caldwell, Janis Donnaud, Erik German, Irene Noguchi, Stephanie Paterik, Solana Pyne, Liesl Schwabe, and Jessica Seigel.

Thanks also to Justin Barton for his patience, his encouragement, his singular ability to distill life to its essence, and his love.

About the Author

Corinne Purtill is a journalist. She lives in California with her family.

Made in United States
North Haven, CT
21 August 2022

22921978R00093